PRAISE for Heaven is a Garden

"Jan Johnsen touches my soul with her insights on gardens, as well as on living life. You'll be touched too as she teaches you how to create a divine, unhurried landscape with simplicity, sanctuary and delight."

~ Jim Peterson, Publisher, *Garden Design* Magazine

"In Heaven is a Garden *we take a voyage into the sublime heart of nature's delights. Jan Johnsen guides us all into a flock of colors, heavenly textures, and the eternal wheel of the cosmos streaming into us from head to toe. To walk in Jan's gardens is to capture nature by seeing more than you can remember and remembering more than you can see."*

~ Travis L. Price III, FAIA, architect, author of *The Mythic Modern*

"Mixing little known, fascinating facts with a sense of wonder about the environment, Jan Johnsen guides us through proven techniques to infuse serenity in our gardens. She begins with an explanation of three simple words: simplicity, sanctuary, and delight – the basis for creating gardens that inspire us and provide a place for reflection. With so many other good suggestions in this book as well, anyone who designs gardens should have this book on their resource shelf."

~ Vanessa Gardner Nagel, designer, author, Director of Communications, Association of Professional Landscape Designers

"Heaven is a Garden transports the reader with an exquisite combination of ancient garden design principles and twenty-first century creativity and innovation. A definite must for every nature and garden enthusiast."

~ Bente Hansen, author, energy healer

"Heaven is a garden, and similarly, a garden is heaven. Jan Johnsen brought heaven, beauty and tranquility to my own garden. She's the best!"

~ John T. Mickel, Curator of Ferns Emeritus, New York Botanical Garden; Author of *Ferns for American Gardens*

Heaven *is a* Garden

Heaven *is a* Garden

Designing Serene Outdoor Spaces
for Inspiration and Reflection

Jan Johnsen

st. lynn's
press

PITTSBURGH

Heaven is a Garden
Designing Serene Spaces for Inspiration and Reflection

ISBN-13: 978-0-9855622-9-8

Library of Congress Control Number: 2013941491
CIP information available upon request

First Edition, 2014

St. Lynn's Press . POB 18680 . Pittsburgh, PA 15236
412.466.0790 . www.stlynnspress.com

Book design – Holly Rosborough
Editor – Catherine Dees

All photos © Jan Johnsen, with the exception of the following:
Berkshire Botanical Garden, pages 51, 52; Diane Burdick, page 17, upper left;
Caitlin Jean, page 83; Laura McKillop, pages 56 (upper l.), 84, 90, 92, 101;
Courtesy of PWP Landscape Architecture, p. 68; Sam Rebben, page 87.

Illustrations on pages 39, 40 and 67 by Laura McKillop.

Printed in Canada
On certified FSC recycled paper using soy-based inks

This title and all of St. Lynn's Press books may be purchased for educational, business or sales promotional use. For information please write:
Special Markets Department . St. Lynn's Press . POB 18680 . Pittsburgh, PA 15236

10 9 8 7 6 5 4 3 2 1

To all the gardeners
past and present
who share their love
of Nature with others
in the best way they can…

Table of Contents

* * *

Introduction

The glory of the garden lies in
more than meets the eye.

– Rudyard Kipling

*H*ave you ever experienced a moment when the wafting fragrance of flower blossoms captured your attention and lifted you away? Or when the birdsong around you was louder than the chatter in your head? This exquisite moment of stillness is what I call "stop time," and it can occur anywhere and any time: while basking in the warm morning sun, gardening, or even as you hurry to your car! At these times, you may have paused, breathed in the fragrant air, enjoyed the trilling of the birds and felt a connection, for that instant, to the green world around you.

The boxwood bordering this patio adds a feeling of enclosure. The artful bench in the background acts as a visual focal point.

What if you knew that you could experience moments like this for the asking – that you could create your own outdoor environment to encourage such deep connections, such restorative reveries? In my forty years of transforming ordinary, even nondescript, sites into compelling landscapes, I have seen how light, color and trickling waters can work together to offer respite from a busy world and make our hearts sing. Thomas Moore wrote of this power in *The Re-enchantment of Everyday Life*: "Today we look for healing and renewal in the offices of physicians and therapists, when we could be out looking for holy wells and enchanted groves that fortify the soul with their natural mysteries." We may not all have holy wells at our disposal, but we can come close; we might even discover that when we plant trees with an awareness of their ancient purposes we are inviting an enchanted grove into our midst – a place that strengthens our wellbeing and inspires quiet reflection. A place that takes us outside of time.

The design ideas you will encounter in this book are a blend of modern and traditional practices, some that go back thousands of years. I have found that mixing contemporary taste with historic design approaches makes a garden more relaxing and encourages that magical "stop time" we all desire. It allows us to enter into an unhurried state of mind, no matter what is going on beyond our garden gate.

My fascination with plants began early in life, even though I grew up in the concrete environment of New York City apartments. In high school I won the Manhattan Science Fair with an experiment on the effect of sound on the growth of plants. My premise, those many years ago, was that high-pitched sounds help plants grow. It seemed slightly absurd then, but now, scientists have determined that the high frequency vibrations of birdsong help to open up the pores on plant leaves so that they absorb more nutrients and grow more rapidly. In effect, the sound of birdsong stimulates plants to grow faster!

As a college student I lived in Kyoto, Japan, and worked at a high-pressure architecture office in Osaka. On weekends, I would visit the famous Japanese gardens and it was there that I found my calling. As I walked the green, mossy pathways and breathed in the cedar-scented air, my mind would clear and I felt stress melt away. This experience opened my eyes to the restorative powers of serene gardens. I saw what sublime peace could be had even in a small garden within an urban environment. I subsequently went to work in a Japanese landscape architecture office and left to study landscape architecture at the University of Hawaii.

This mossy path symbolizes a journey and the forks in the road we all face.

Flower planters on steps add a colorful punch. The soft flowers against the stone are a lovely contrast. The wall light highlights the flowers at night.

Heaven is a Garden is an introduction to the key elements that make a landscape feel balanced and harmonious. Some of the elements are so much a part of our lives – like trees and rocks – that we may not have actually paid attention to them before, or realized what kind of subliminal effects they have on us. So, perhaps this book will serve as a re-introduction to some of the wonders that exist all around us in Nature, just waiting for our eyes to truly see them. To bring you from concept to application, I'll be offering suggestions of specific practices and plants that I have found work well together to evoke a deep sense of serenity.

My exposure to many cultures began a life-long study of how our forebears interacted with Nature. I learned that the Celts and Japanese honored certain trees, that the Greeks used the golden ratio in their designs and that water in a garden lifts the spirits. In this book, I share these insights with you, and many more. I hope that it may prompt you to see the outdoors a little differently. For instance, once you know why east is considered auspicious in many traditions, you will never site a gate or a garden bed without this cardinal direction in mind!

In these pages you will find chapters that explore each of these key landscaping elements:

- The Power of Place considers the ways terrain can be molded and accented to create sanctuary and meaning.
- Creating Music for the Eye shows how shape, line and proportion can unify a garden.
- Calling on the Trees addresses the enlivening influence of our arboreal friends by deciphering the language of the trees.

- The Magic of Water delves into water's mystery and the many ways it enhances an outdoor environment.
- A Rock's Resonance explores the powerfully evocative qualities of stone.
- Color – Nature's Catalyst reveals the therapeutic effects of color and light in a garden design.

Many of the photographs in the book were taken in gardens I have designed. I have intentionally kept the text to a minimum to allow the photographs to speak for me as much as possible. I believe, as Shakespeare wrote, that we can "...find tongues in trees, books in running brooks, sermons in stones, and good in everything..." (*As You Like It*).

It is my hope that *Heaven is a Garden* will help you hear those sermons as well. Whether you are an individual intending to create a beautiful backyard garden, a landscape architect or designer wishing to expand your ideas for your clients, or someone who is just thinking about designing a dream garden, this book will give you insights to help you create a glorious outdoor space – perfect for inspiration and reflection. 🌿

The timeless appeal of dainty flowers against stone.
A planting pocket within the wall is a good way to do this.

The Power of Place

Consult the genius of the place in all.
– Alexander Pope

A "heavenly" garden stills the world and holds you in its embrace. As you walk beneath leafy canopies or beside colorful flowers, wellbeing's cloud envelops you and the stress of modern life slowly drops away. This garden has little to do with its size and everything to do with the emotional connection it makes with you. Your garden paradise can be as simple as a sun-dappled deck overlooking a small cascade or a homey terrace filled with planters and statuary.

It can be an expanse of lawn bordered with exuberant flowers or a rustic scene of native plants and rock outcrops. Whatever your vision of a heavenly garden, it should fulfill your desire for a private space where you can enjoy Nature's glory – where you can breathe and just be. Nowhere else do we feel as uplifted as when we are in a setting designed for relaxation and contemplation. Another way of describing such a place is "an unhurried garden."

I love to create long, sweeping grass steps as these shown here. They are simple, gracious and relatively easy to install.

A heavenly, unhurried garden should be designed with three basic features in mind: simplicity, sanctuary and delight. Let me start with those three lovely words and show you what I mean.

Simplicity. When you have economy of form and line in a garden, the effect is calming and restful. A good example of this is a gently undulating plant bed. Its sweeping lines are relaxing and – though simple – can be as compelling as a rectilinear formal garden. "Less is more" is the rule here.

Sanctuary. Have you ever noticed that the most desirable place to sit outdoors is with your back to a wall or a tall hedge and looking at a lovely view? The security you feel in such a protected area is what I term "sanctuary." It is the draw of a shaded walk, the call of a hidden gazebo or quiet niche. It is the lure of the sheltered corner.

A low, semi-circular retaining wall and a rock garden creates a sheltered feeling of sanctuary.

Delight. Delight is anything that gladdens your heart: a hollowed out tree trunk, an interesting gate or an elegant stone lion. It is the most personal aspect of a heavenly outdoor space and can be found amidst a patio flush with planters or in a woodland garden dotted with foamflowers and ferns. You may thrill to a fire pit or bubbling fountain. Delight prompts you to savor your surroundings.

Delight in a garden can come in many forms. Multi-colored tulips, a deep blue gate flanked by boxwood, a rustic cascade or a line of the exuberant and hardy 'Disco Belle Pink' hibiscus *(Hibiscus moscheutos* 'Disco Belle Pink'*)*.

These three underlying ideas can be incorporated into any garden, no matter the style or setting. With the mantra of "simplicity, sanctuary and delight," you can go ahead and take the first steps in creating a serenely beautiful landscape.

After I created this intimate corner, the property owner placed what we call a "pod" here. A perfect place to enjoy the garden!

Finding the Power Spot – Drama in a Garden

When I begin a garden design, I always look first for the site's "power spot." This is a place that, for some reason, seems a little more interesting than anywhere else. A high section of lawn, a shaded corner or a half hidden rock can become the anointed power spot in your garden. You can strengthen or dilute a site's character by highlighting its power spot.

In order to determine where it is, I walk around and consider the dominant features of the land. I stand quietly in different areas and feel the mood each one generates. Elevated locations, such as the top of a steep slope or an outlook, can elicit "a sensation, dwarfing yet ennobling," writes Derek Clifford in *The History of Garden Design*. But a power spot doesn't need to be grand; it can be a shaded area in a corner. This is a more subdued and familiar kind; it feels comfortable, like a favorite sweater.

If you are wondering where a power spot is on your property, please know that there is no one correct answer. It is your particular translation of the "genius of the place" that is important. The area that appeals to you the most will undoubtedly speak to others as well. You may see treasure in that slight rise or be attracted to a particular rock. My advice is, Go ahead and highlight it! Clear around it, illuminate it or make a small path that leads to it so friends can enjoy it. Once they ascend to the top of a cleared slope or sit on a swing beneath a great tree, they will understand why you call it your power spot.

An overlooked, rocky site can become a power spot. Place a statue, sculpture or light here.

Seven Ways to Highlight a Power Spot in a Garden

1. **Name it!** Naming something makes it special. Descriptive monikers are a fun way to mark areas of a garden. For example, you might call a massive tree that stands solitary in a field The Lonesome Oak. A promontory with a vista can become Lookout Point and a Japanese landscape featuring a statue might be referred to as The Buddha Garden.

The presence of a statue can help in naming a garden.

2. **Mark the spot.** Place a sign, a marker or an art piece here to signify the area. It can be as elemental as an upright stone.

3. **Place a bench here.** Benches or rustic sitting rocks establish a power spot as a destination. The opportunity to sit on a bench always draws people. A view of a curved stone bench in the corner of a yard catching the morning sun is irresistible.

Inviting bench in a morning garden.

4. **Make it easy to get to.** A power spot must be accessible. Provide a path to the spot, even if it is only a strip of mowed grass or a small stepping stone walk, six feet long. If you build it, they will follow!

5. **Add seasonal interest.** The colors of the season add punch to a power spot. A simple splash of Coleus injects excitement in the summer and continues through the fall.

'Sedona' coleus adds a spot of seasonal color.

6. **Add lighting.** Outdoor lights or battery-powered candles in lanterns provide sparkle and add intrigue. They invite visitors to enjoy a garden at day's end.

7. **Maintain it.** Fallen branches, litter or brushy overgrowth can take away from the enjoyment of your power spot. A little natural imperfection is fine, but try to keep the area fairly free of debris.

The Draw of a High Point

A lookout is one of the most exciting areas in a landscape. The top of a hill, a rock or any other kind of high point satisfies our instinctive desire for a prospect, where we can view our surroundings. The higher the promontory, the better the view and the more connected we feel to the overall scene. This is what makes a high point so universally appealing. The gazebo shown at left was placed on a high point for that reason.

Thomas Jefferson knew about the power of a high vantage point. He purposely built his famous home, Monticello, upon a lofty summit in Virginia and wrote eloquently about enjoying the view. In a 1786 letter to Maria Cosway, he wrote that from his perch he could look down "into the workhouse of nature, to see her clouds, hail, snow, rain, thunder, all fabricated at our feet!" Indeed, given a choice between sitting on a low portion of a lawn or a place farther up, most of us will invariably choose to sit uphill. Perhaps it is an inborn instinct that we all have.

A lookout in the landscape draws people to it. I placed this custom-designed gazebo on a high point so people could look down on the garden below.

I often enhance an existing high point by creating a "destination" there. A small area at the top of a slope can be leveled and retained with a low wall, as shown in the photo at left, opposite page. Such a cut-and-fill approach can provide a place large enough for a gazebo, a bench or some comfortable chairs. The view of a garden seat on a hill acts as a compelling destination and visitors will look for a way to get there. Their prize, upon arrival, is a comfortable perch from which to enjoy the summit.

I created this enticing place to sit by levelling out a slope. The low wall in front retains the level area. I then chose some wonderful outdoor seats to add a bit of fun.

Long grassed steps make a slope seem less steep. I used split Belgian Blocks as the risers here. I also made sure to alter the direction of the top run of steps to prevent a monotonous, overwhelming effect.

In the garden shown here, I painted two new benches a dark green to make them less obtrusive and to blend in with the scene.

A Graceful Way Up to a High Point

People often see a climb up a hill to a high point as an obstacle, but you can make it a lovely winding path or a mysterious rustic ascent. Both treatments transform an arduous journey into an enjoyable experience. In the case of very steep inclines, I rely on the illusion of scale and proportion to make it seem less intimidating. My motto

is, "The higher the hill, the longer the steps," because I have found that a long line of steps cutting across a slope reduces its perceived steepness. In the garden shown above, I installed three sets of long grass steps with split cobblestone risers across the face of a slope. The 12-foot-long steps counter the tallness of the hill and make it seem almost ceremonial. In fact, the formality of the grass steps so impressed my clients' daughter that she chose to have her outdoor wedding ceremony here on these steps a year after they were installed.

Curved grass steps create a lovely line in a garden. Here I made the steps exceptionally wide for a gracious effect.

I first saw steps with grassed treads in the Dumbarton Oaks estate in Washington, DC, 35 years ago. This garden is open to the public, and I heartily encourage you to visit there. The steps were designed by Beatrix Farrand in the early part of the 20th century and hark back to the grassed treads of English gardens. Since then, I have used them so often that grass steps have become a signature feature of my garden designs. I have found that they can be used in landscape styles ranging from contemporary to cottage. While the treads are always lawn, the risers of the steps can be fashioned from Belgian blocks, bluestone pavers set upright, thin granite edging or Corten steel.

Beatrix Farrand, Landscape Gardener

Beatrix Farrand, 1872-1959, was America's first female landscape architect. She was responsible for designing the grounds of Princeton, Yale and many estate gardens, and assisted in plantings at the White House. Her masterpiece was Dumbarton Oaks, in the Georgetown section of Washington, DC.

Farrand grew up when there were no schools of landscape architecture, so she apprenticed herself to Charles Sprague Sargent, founder of Harvard University's Arnold Arboretum and made several tours of Europe's great gardens. She had an intuitive eye for design and this skill, together with her horticultural knowledge, helped her build a thriving practice.

In 1921, Farrand was hired by Mildred and Robert Bliss to design the gardens of Dumbarton Oaks. Mrs. Bliss wanted a romantic garden and requested that all details in the seats, ornaments and gates have literary connections. The ten-acre property is a series of separate outdoor areas connected by walkways. Long views are numerous because Farrand believed in offering beautiful vistas on which to gaze.

As a token of their gratitude, the Blisses placed a plaque dedicated to Beatrix in the garden. It is in Latin and reads:

"May kindly stars guide the dreams born beneath
The spreading branches of Dumbarton Oaks.
Dedicated to the friendship of Beatrix Farrand
And to successive generations of seekers after Truth."

The elegance and versatility of grass steps enables them to be sweeping arcs or a contemporary rectilinear feature. The type of line you choose for your garden depends on your intent. Long gracious curves allow people to fan out in all directions while straight lines of steps channel visitors toward a desired route. Curving steps look good from all angles, but straight steps are best viewed from the front. The depth of your grass treads can also vary: the minimum depth is 18 inches, but they can be as deep as 42 inches. I sometimes slope the treads so that they become, in effect, a ramped stairway. This aids in drainage for the grass and requires fewer steps to ascend a hill. The important point to remember, however, is that deeper steps require lower risers for a comfortable ascent.

Using "Hide and Reveal" to Lead to a High Point

An ascent to a high point can be made more enticing when you use an ancient Japanese garden design technique known as *miegakure* or "hide and reveal." It rests on the idea that hiding a full view of a space can make it seem larger than it is. It can also make an ascent seem less daunting. Thus, if you screen a section of steps, visitors are more likely to venture up to see what is out of sight.

I "hide and reveal" steps by angling sections of them within a long run. A bend in a series of steps makes the ascent seem less steep and heightens the air of mystery. A small landing at each bend is helpful and lets people enjoy a meditative pause. I also obscure the full view up a hill by placing a leafy plant strategically, using shadows to "hide" a portion of the steps or narrowing them near the top.

Of course, outdoor steps that are half hidden should be illuminated at night. You can place lights high up in overhead tree branches to provide a diffuse "moonlight" effect; this creates quite the romantic scene in the evening. Additionally, a decorative light fixture such as a stone lantern next to the steps acts as a striking garden feature as well as a safety beacon.

The ascent to a high point is a significant aspect of its power spot appeal. The walk up may be narrow, rocky steps, a gracious incline or a grand staircase. Whichever it is, it will certainly be a lovely part of the serene garden experience.

The ascent to a high point is a significant aspect of its "power spot" appeal. These are various steps I have created to draw people up to a high point. Each fits the setting.

The Elizabethan "Snail Mount"

If you relish the idea of having a high point in the garden but your land is relatively level, why not follow historic tradition and mold an artificial hill? The first known constructed "mountain" was the legendary Hanging Gardens of Babylon. Towering over the sun-baked plains of Mesopotamia, this eight-story-high complex of terraced gardens was sculpted from imported soil and meant to evoke the tree-covered mountains of a far-off country. A more modest idea – and one more suitable for today's gardens – is a variation on the lovely Elizabethan "snail mount," which was a popular outdoor feature in the 17th century.

In 1625, English philosopher Francis Bacon wrote in his "Essay of Gardens" about forming a high "mount" in the center of a landscape: "I wish also, in the very middle, a fair mount, with three ascents and alleys enough for four to walk abreast; which I would have to be perfect circles...; and the whole mount to be thirty foot high."

Visitors would walk up a three-story grassy hill via a path spiraling around to the top. The walk would cut into the mound, making it look like a snail shell, thus the name "snail mount." The gradual ascent, going round and round, was perfect for ladies in their stiff hoop skirts. Their climb was rewarded at the top with a view of the formal gardens below. A power spot indeed! I suspect that another reason for creating a snail mount may have come from the availability of excess soil that was generated from the creation of the water features and sunken gardens popular during this time.

A Quiet Power Spot

The lookout reigns over a garden, but the shadowy niche nestles within its heart. This kind of quiet power spot is "a place to dream and linger in of a summer evening, green with perpetual verdure." So wrote the American poet and author Hildegarde Hawthorne in *The Lure of the Garden.* Such a place becomes a sweet outdoor sanctuary, as in the seclusion experienced under a wisteria-covered arbor, beneath the canopy of a wide-spreading apple tree or beside a ferny

A shady spot and a secret path enhances a power spot.

grotto. Interestingly, a garden that contains both a bright open area and a muted, shady

This was a shady spot that I enhanced with a stepping stone path, ostrich ferns, and a rock bordered dry stream that serves as a seasonal drainage feature. Sustainable, functional and lovely – a quiet power spot indeed!

spot makes for the most appealing locale, as it blends two distinct atmospheres. Imagine, for example, sitting on a bench under the protective canopy of a tree and looking out onto an open sunny lawn.

A Woodland "Folly"

Shady corners can become power spots if you enhance them in some way. You can do this simply by clearing brush away from around a large tree or placing an art piece in a forgotten corner or niche among plants. I was once asked to draw attention to a shady spot at the edge of a distant wooded hillside. It could be seen from the house and the property owner suggested I design a folly for this neglected area. A folly is a picturesque feature, an eye-catching decora-

tive element. They were common in 18th century European landscapes and were often built in the form of Roman temples or ruins, placed atop a faraway hill on an estate or set in a wooded hollow.

Following this time-honored tradition, I set four cast stone columns in an arc in a leveled area of my client's garden. I used four columns and four curved grass steps to define the front of the folly. In many traditions, the number 4 represents the Earth, and so groupings of four elements are considered very stable and grounding. I retained the hill behind with large rocks and planted low growing pachysandra around them. This evergreen ground cover plant forms a dark green backdrop behind the light colored columns, evoking a rustic elegance amidst wooded surroundings. A shady corner power spot, indeed!

Four cast stone columns help to "ground" the scene.

A Garden in Tune with the Four Directions

In this age of GPS navigation, the cardinal directions of North, South, East and West may seem nothing more than useful aspects of highway signs. But in ages past, the "Four Winds," as the directions were called, were an important consideration when laying out buildings, towns and gardens. For example, the main shopping road of ancient Roman towns was called the *cardo,* or heart, and always ran in a north/south direction. This tenet of town planning can still be seen in New York's Fifth Avenue and other prominent avenues of older cities.

Using the Qualities of North, South, East and West

Each of the cardinal directions can be thought of as having its own distinct qualities, based on their solar and geomagnetic characteristics. In fact, many cultures saw them as having particular personalities. North is solid and quiet while South is celebratory and expansive. East is fruitful and promotes growth and West is social. If you know the characteristics of each direction you can knowledgeably locate a bench, house or plant bed.

The Four Directions in Brief

North. The direction of wisdom and contemplation. A site on the north side is the best location for an artful viewing garden.

East. The direction of growth and rejuvenation. Vegetable gardens prosper here. Thoughtful reveries are best done facing east.

South. Celebratory and vibrant. The south side of a home is the natural place for an open lawn and flower gardens.

West. The direction of expression and sharing. A west-facing patio shaded by trees is best for gatherings with others.

North – The Direction of Earthy Contemplation

North is the direction of all things that relate to the earth. It is associated with quiet contemplation and meditative sculpture gardens. The north side of a house is the natural place for large stones, specimen trees and any artful item that is to be admired quietly. We look to the north for "grounding."

Why is this? In the early 1990s, scientists discovered that our brains contained a biomineral called magnetite. This highly magnetic form of

I placed these granite *steles* in this garden on the north side of a house. They act as a focal point from a large foyer window.

iron oxide is similar to the magnetite naturally found in rocks. Sailors and ancient seafarers called it a lodestone; they would rub magnetite-laden rocks on metal needles to magnetize them. This was the genesis of the directional compass where the needles always point north. The magnetite in our brain is like our personal lodestone and may make us respond to the subtle magnetic pull of north. Perhaps this is why some feng shui practitioners advise us to sleep with our head pointing north!

Knowing that stone of any sort befits the north side of a house, I designed a quiet garden

of stone and grasses for a contemporary home with a large, north-facing window. The floor to ceiling window offered a long, narrow view and reminded me of a Japanese alcove, where a flower arrangement or art piece is displayed.

I placed five rough *steles,* or upright stones, amidst soft, ornamental grasses in a plant bed at the far end of a long view (photo at left). The bed is edged by thin bluestone pavers and sits beyond a field of smooth, tawny colored concrete slabs and gray crushed stone. The contrast of the stone, concrete and feathery grasses provides an interesting textural counterpoint. The stones are particularly stunning at night when underground "well lights" dramatically up-light each one. The diffuse light spills over onto the surrounding grasses, forming an ethereal sight.

Several varieties of grasses are planted here. The feathery dwarf fountain grass *(Pennisetum alopecuroides* 'Hameln') and maiden grass *(Miscanthus sinensis gracillimus)* are wonderful companions to the short but vibrant 'Elijah Blue' fescue *(Festuca glauca* 'Elijah Blue').

The soft blades of 'Elijah Blue' blue fescue look great next to a native glacial rock outcrop.

An important pointer for North gardens is to remember that shadows fall on the north side of a building. This can cast an unappealing gloom on a scene. Therefore, I located this garden about 20 feet out from the building – beyond the reach of the long shadows of winter. The resulting long view also adds drama and depth to the scene. A wonderful bonus for north-facing gardens is that at midday the sun is always behind you, which ensures that "nature's spotlight" shines on the object but never gets in your eyes.

A bench catches the gentle morning sun coming from the east. The 'Neon Lights' foam-flowers (Tiarella 'Neon Lights') that bloom in spring like it too.

East, the Auspicious Direction

East, the home of the early morning sun, is considered by many cultures to be the auspicious cardinal direction. Wise gardeners site their vegetables plots facing east because morning light provides optimal plant growth. Yoga practitioners face east when performing morning Salute to the Sun exercises to bask in the sun's enlivening eastern rays. Designers of Gothic cathedrals sited them so congregants face east for prayers. And many libraries of old were designed so that the majority of their windows faced east.

We know east is associated with morning sunlight, but why do historic traditions also connect it with intellectual and spiritual pursuits?

A viewing garden for the north side of a house, far out of reach of winter shadows.

A hammock can encourage daydreaming, especially when it faces the east.

Knowledgeable garden designers, aware that an eastern outlook may enhance mental acuity, locate benches so that they face that direction. Ideally, you might encourage better daydreaming by hanging a hammock to catch the rays of the eastern sun. And if the hammock's eastern orientation is coupled with a stand of trees to the west, then it is also shaded from the hot afternoon sun.

Always Follow the Light. There is nothing quite as pleasing as morning light shining through an east-facing garden gate. As we enter we see the brightness beckoning to us beyond the portal. The idea of the sun being in front of us, drawing us in, is similar to the "moth theory" of the 20th-century Miami Beach hotel architect Morris Lapidus, who noted that people, like moths, are attracted to light. This reasoning may be the basis of the "law of orientation" in Indian Vastu (like Chinese feng shui) which recommends that front doors, town entrances and garden gates all face east.

Morning sun streams through this gate, lighting up the dappled willow (Salix integra Hakuro-nishiki) that is planted just beyond it.

It may have to do with the effect of direction on our brain. Neuroscientist Dr. Tony Nader asserts that when we face east the firing patterns of the neurons in our brain's thalamus are more coherent than when we face south or west. Could it be that we think more clearly facing east? Vastu, the ancient Indian system concerned with the design of the physical environment, suggests that students should face east when studying, for better concentration and sharper memory.

In fact, the word *orientation* means towards the Orient, or towards the east.

An east-facing gate directs the morning light to highlight whatever is near the entrance. I used this to great effect when I designed this tall gate and

An east-facing gate directs the view within.

stone columns. The 6-foot high arched gate, flanked on both sides by tall pillars, faces east; in the morning, the sun's rays travel through it, spotlighting a golden thread leaf False Cypress tree *(Chamaecyparis pisifera* 'Filifera Aurea'*)*. The lighting effect is enticing.

South - The Direction of Celebration and Flowers

South is the home of the midday sun and, according to feng shui principles, is the direction that resonates with radiance and light. The south part of a property is the natural place for an open field, a large lawn or a flower garden. It is a good spot for celebrations and can feature strong colors such as red and purple in brightly

colored banners or foliage. A border of hot colors – yellow, orange, red – also looks wonderful in a south-facing garden.

The south side of a building or property is also well suited for anything to do with light or fire. It is direction of the fire element in feng shui; therefore, a garden torch, light fixture, fire pit or barbeque is at home here. Interestingly, Vastu considers land that is elevated in the south and southwest to be the kind of terrain that bestows prosperity.

The South Lawn of the White House uses the qualities of the south perfectly. The expansive lawn is situated south of the President's

An open south-facing area features sun–loving Knock Out® roses, ornamental grasses and Sargent's juniper *(Juniperus chinensis* var. *sargentii)*. The south part of a property is the natural place for celebrations and flower gardens.

West is the direction for outdoor gatherings at the end of a day. I designed this west-facing patio to enjoy the view and the late afternoon.

Residence and is used for official outdoor events like the state arrival ceremony and the annual egg-rolling contest, as well as informal barbecues. Thomas Jefferson graded the South Lawn and built mounds on either side of it, which direct a visitor's view down a long south-facing axis.

West – The Direction of "Name and Fame"

West is the direction of the setting sun and is associated with the end of the day and fellowship. High-canopied trees that lightly shade the west side of a house create the sweetest place to linger at the end of the day. In Vastu, the west is where "name and fame are made" – in other words, where we share time with friends. A "sunset terrace" basking in the long orange-red rays of the setting sun is the best place for socializing.

Water is also associated with west. The trickling water from a fountain cools the atmosphere on a sunny west-facing patio. The photo at right shows a fountain I designed that features shows a series of dramatic fountainheads along a western stone wall directing streams of water into a raised stone basin.

The colors that look especially vibrant in the west are rich reds and dark orange.

Follow "The Way of the Sun." West is the direction of endings, so it makes sense that garden walks proceed in a "sunwise" or clockwise direction. Visitors travel a garden path from east to west, following the sun's path in the sky. This is akin to the Hindu practice of circumambulation, where they circle special places in a clockwise direction. The reason for this circular walk has been attributed to symbolic causes, but I surmise

Water features are well suited for west-facing sites.

I laid out this stepped garden path so that it curves out of sight and invites you to walk toward the sunlight.

that it may be due to the flow of geomagnetic forces. Just as an electrical generator works with a rotating coil to create a magnetic field, it may be that people walking in a circular motion intensifies the geomagnetic energy field within that space.

A loop path allows people to walk the perimeter of a garden, looking inward from different viewpoints (photo, left). You can place different garden elements along this encircling path, creating places where people might pause. The stopping points lead people from one destination point to the next, bringing them back to where they began. The walk may be paved, gravel, grassed or mulched – or a combination of all.

"Pooling and Channeling"

In order to encourage people to pause on a loop path or any walk through a landscape, I use a design technique called "pooling and channeling." It is based on the idea that people move through a space in the same way that water flows: water moves rapidly through a narrow, straight channel but slows down when it enters into a larger, wider pool. Similarly, people tend to pause when they arrive in an open area. So, to encourage people to slow down, make a larger area along a walk or where two narrow paths meet. People will instinctively stop here.

A Focus on Place

The highest expression of "place" comes from honoring the natural environs of a region, taking a cue from natural scenes and using native rocks and plants. This should be the basis of any garden. Wherever you live – in the moist Northwest, the southern high desert, the Mediterranean Pacific coast or the lush South – I encourage you to incorporate native plants in your garden design. For example, if you live in the Northeast of the United States, observe the glory of the eastern woodlands. If you live in hot, dry Southern California, then succulents, agaves

Native plants are the highest expression of a place.

and cacti may be your theme. Swaths of native flowers, shrubs and grasses provide an entrancing vision that encompasses the beauty of shifting seasons and feeds and houses the ecosystem's birds, bees and more. In addition, local stones and plant material "resonate" with their environ- ment, lending a harmonious atmosphere to a garden. For all these reasons, try to use native or local resources whenever you can.

Melding local stones with existing vegetation enriches a garden and its connection to "place".

Garden Metaphors

This shady dry stream suggests a river and catches stormwater when it rains heavily. Every year we plant annual flowers among the hostas, oakleaf hydrangeas and Japanese painted fern to make it colorfully eye-catching.

A garden metaphor is what I call any landscape feature that recre- ates a scene of natural beauty in a smaller scale. This can include a dry stone stream to suggest a river, a small earth mound to represent a mountain, or a grouping of trees to evoke a forest.

The ancient Japanese garden makers elevated recreating natural scenes to a high art. Their honored 11th-century manual on garden making, *Sakuteiki,* says that "you should design each part of the garden tastefully, recalling your memories of how nature presented itself for each feature…Think over the famous places of scenic beauty throughout the land, and design your garden with the mood of harmony, modeling after the general air of such places."

My favorite garden metaphor is a dry stream. It connotes a babbling brook but, for the most part, contains no water. I was first introduced to dry streams when I lived in Kyoto, the locale of most of Japan's famous gardens. I fell in love with their versatility and I use them often in my landscapes. I create a dry stream by lining a curving trench with rocks, buried halfway into the earth. The trench is filled with gravel and topped with a thin layer of smooth, rounded stones. Dry streams can be a prominent and beautiful feature in the garden while effectively dealing with seasonal wetness – you can incorporate subsurface pipes and sump pumps beneath their beautiful exterior to help out with surface drainage.

Plantings for a Dry Stream

I created a dry stream in my small backyard. It adds a serene touch and looks great studded with a variety of plants. Because the dry stream forms a primary view from the house, I tried to follow the Japanese garden rule in planting it up: approximately 30 percent of the plants are deciduous and 70 percent are evergreen. The abundance of evergreen plants keeps the stream from looking desolate in the winter.

*I chose mostly low maintenance plants that tolerate partial shade. The list includes Japanese garden juniper (*Juniperus procumbens *'nana'), 'Ice Dance' sedge (*Carex *'Ice Dance'), Golden Sedge (*Carex oshimensis *'Evergold'), Siberian iris 'Caesar's Brother' (*Iris sibirica *'Caesar's Brother'), hemlock trees (*Tsuga canadensis), arborvitae trees (*Thuja occidentalis *'Emerald') and dwarf fountain grass (*Pennistum alopecuroides *'Hameln'). For summer color, I plant the wonderful, drought tolerant, purple annual strawflower, Globe Amaranth 'Buddy' (*Gomphrena globosa *'Buddy'). By the way, most of these plants are deer resistant!*

I love my backyard dry stream. It adds garden interest to a small space and I feel at peace when I look upon it.

Fencing an Outdoor Space:
The Inner Sanctum

A fence or screen transforms an ordinary outdoor space into a personal area where you can enjoy the outdoors undisturbed. A beautiful fence can

This distinctive gate was fashioned from a salvaged window grill

define a garden, add a sense of privacy and make it seem like a "place apart." The psychological buffer it provides satisfies our instinctive desire for security and, if designed correctly, increases the allure of an outdoor patio or garden.

Our ancestors would often enclose places of natural beauty such as a gurgling spring or forest clearing with a rudimentary enclosure. This provided needed protection from enemies and created a special place to relax and enjoy shade, refreshment and camaraderie. You can do the same, but make sure to place a fence far enough away from a sitting area so you don't feel penned in. Soften the fence's presence and take care to place the gate so that it does not interrupt the flow within the space. And lastly, choose the layout of the fence carefully.

The "Insulation" of a Wall

Walls create the outdoor sanctuary that we crave, offering an extra layer of insulation to a garden. They are the bones of a garden, dividing and defining space and creating sheltered outdoor areas. A tall stone wall framing one side of an outdoor space can act as a magnet. Place a few chairs in front of such a wall and arrange a collection of colorful planters and you have a delightful area to enjoy with friends.

I designed this patio to be partially enclosed by a low wall to afford a feeling of protection.

These two stone walls retain a steep slope and, at the same time, make a great backdrop.

In the photo shown here, I added a lower stone wall in front of an existing stone wall, to retain a high hill. The lower wall is not too high and creates an inviting space more in proportion. I placed three long bluestone steps leading up to this raised terrace. The strong horizontal lines of the steps visually counterbalance the steepness of the hill.

I often partially enclose an outdoor area with a low sitting wall, no higher than 22 inches. It makes a space feel intimate yet is not confining. Both rectangular and curved patios can be partially bordered with a wall. I have found that walls with right angle corners accommodate large furniture arrangements and are well suited to formal

Low walls create interesting lines in a landscape and form inviting niches. This allows people to sit undisturbed and out of the way of people passing by.

or modern gardens. On the other hand, curved walls bordering free form patio spaces create an alluring line and add a more playful tone.

In the garden shown below left, I deliberately created a 15-foot-long niche bordered by a 21-inch-high wall in which to place furniture. Niches are the ultimate example of an insulated space, providing a coziness that is often missing in large, expansive landscapes. The stone wall is uncapped because the modern vernacular calls for simple lines and a minimum of ornamental detail.

* * *

The Power of Place lies in the ways that our physical environment affects us so mysteriously. For this reason, the spirit of a place must always be considered first and foremost. But what about the impact of line and shape? This often-overlooked aspect of a garden can radically alter the quality of our experience within it. The next chapter considers the intangible gifts we receive when pathways, terraces, plant beds and more are created with knowing attention to line and shape. You will see that the discussion of lyrical lines, repetition and contrast seem to evoke music. So much so, that I am encouraged to refer to line and shape in a garden as "Music for the Eye." 🌿

TWO

Creating Music for the Eye: Line and Shape

*Design is not making beauty; beauty emerges from
selection, affinities, integration, and love.*
– Louis Kahn, architect

*I*f you are fortunate, you have had the experience of walking in a garden and feeling a wave of peace and harmony wash over you. That lovely sensation is partially a response to the shapes and lines within an overall space. The curve of a walk or the shape of a plant bed speaks to us silently. A wonderful example of this is the rose garden at the historic estate Naumkeag,

in Stockbridge, Massachusetts. This landscape of parallel curving paths punctuated by rosebushes was designed by Fletcher Steele in the early 20th century. Its flowing lines imply moving water, and as you look down upon it from a balcony, the marvelous fluidity illustrates how form and line in the landscape can create "music for the eye" (see above). Naumkeag is open to the public.

Curves: the Sinuous Lines of Grace

Naumkeag's unique blue staircase, designed by Fletcher Steele, illustrates the compelling quality of curves in the landscape.

Perhaps the most beguiling shape in a garden is the curving line. It gives an unhurried quality to any outdoor setting. Graceful arcs reflect the forms we see in nature: flower petals, pinecones, leaves and seashells. This similarity is said to have prompted the 18th-century English landscape designer Capability Brown to refer to curves as the "sinuous line of Grace."

Walks, plant beds and walls can all be compelling curved elements in a garden. An undulating walk appears like a meandering stream, a rounded plant bed embraces a lawn and curving walls of any kind make a bold statement. The well-known, curved outdoor staircase at Naumkeag in Stockbridge, Massachusetts, illustrates the appeal of rounded lines beautifully.

One of my favorite walls is at the Storm King Art Center in Mountainville, New York. This extraordinary fieldstone wall, created by Scottish artist Andy Goldsworthy, is 2,278 feet long and was built with native stones gathered from the surrounding woods. The first section of the wall weaves in and out of trees and ends in a sunken pond. It then emerges out from the other side of the pond and leads back uphill. The winding wall links various areas of the property and creates an almost magical atmosphere as people walk alongside it as it travels through field and forest.

Andy Goldsworthy's serpentine fieldstone wall at Storm King Art Center in Mountainville, NY.

Gaudi's Curves

Even the hedges are pruned in curved shapes at Parque Guell in Barcelona

The visionary Barcelona architect of the early 20th century Antonio Gaudí studied the spirals and curves of nature and utilized them in all his projects. Gaudi, unlike other architects of his time, did not rely on rigid shapes, but studied the spirals and curves of Nature and utilized them in all his projects. Consequently, his buildings feature columns spiraling up like trees and ovoid windows peering out onto the world. They are remarkable in their organic glory.

Gaudí's love for curves is on full display in his Parque Güell, a municipal park on the outskirts of Barcelona. Here, he incorporated twisting paths, imaginative colonnades and naturally formed staircases into a steep hillside. The large open public area at the center of the park is surrounded by a long, curving wall and a bench covered with brightly colored broken tiles. The sinuous bench seems to be in constant and colorful motion.

You can also see inventive curves in the unique pruning technique used on hedge plants in Parque Guell. Here, the curve of the benches is reflected in the tops of a carefully trimmed hedge within the landscaped grounds.

The Elasticity of a Curve

Ancient Chinese garden designers used curving perimeter walls to enclose their revered gardens. Osvald Siren described the winding grace of a Chinese garden wall in his book *Gardens of China,* saying, "They seldom follow straight lines, and as a rule are not broken in sharp angles; they rather sweep in wide curves, ascending and descending according to the formation of the ground and thus often have the appearance of being elastic or modeled rather than built up." The elasticity of a curve lends a mysterious air to Chinese gardens.

I laid out this curved stepping stone path in an exaggerated curve to add interest to a simple linkage.

You can use elasticity to pique people's interest by laying out a walkway in a strong, playful line. In the landscape shown in the bottom photo, preceding page, I laid out an S-shaped stepping-stone walk rather than a straightforward access way. The curved walk adds a lyrical quality to the scene and makes the visual experience more interesting. The line of the walk is an integral part of the overall composition rather just a simple linkage.

There are many ways to lay out a curve in a garden. The most common way – laying a garden hose on the ground to make a free-form curve – is my least favorite, because it creates a wriggly shape, the opposite of what a serene garden is all about. It should be about a rhythmic flow of line and form. A more ordered approach is to determine the exact radius of the arc that you would like to create. Then, using a 100-foot tape measure as your compass, mark out a uniformly shaped curve from a central radius point. You can mark the curve on the ground using chalk, marking

Curving grass steps and colorful 'Magic Carpet' roses and dwarf fountain grass make this garden an "unhurried" haven.

paint or a line of powdered limestone, as you pivot around. Such a gentle curve creates a more even "disposition" to the scene.

* * *

In a garden, familiar shapes such as circles, ovals, squares, and spirals affect us in different ways. A circular area is inclusive, drawing us to the center. An oval walk or lawn promotes movement. A spiral plant bed intrigues us. The square is solid and safe, while a triangular space makes us restless and grabs attention. Once you know the impact that recognizable shapes make upon our psyche, you can act as a composer of sorts and use the "melody of form" to make a garden sing.

This curving grassed path is enchanting, especially when the daylilies are in bloom. I placed a "faux bois" (resembling wood) bench by the pond to be a "destination" point.

Circles in the Landscape

I think of the circular form as a "whole note" in the music of a landscape, creating a compelling outdoor feature and fostering unity within its perimeter. We all respond to a shape that has no beginning and no end. A circular patio or plant bed focuses attention inward and almost demands that we look to its central radius point. "The power of the world works in circles, and everything tries to be round," said Black Elk, the great Oglala Sioux spiritual leader (as recounted by John G. Neihardt in *Black Elk Speaks).*

I wanted this area to be a pleasant place to stop and chat so I created a circle and added a low retaining sitting wall around part of its perimeter.

Circular areas can be found everywhere in ancient and traditional landscapes – in Celtic stone ruins, in Native American medicine wheels and Roman amphitheaters. Our predilection for circles carries on into today, as was noted by Christopher Alexander, a professor emeritus of architecture at University of California, Berkeley. In his book, *A Pattern Language,* he writes that we like to relate to each other in circles, and notes that "when people sit down to talk together they try to arrange themselves roughly in a circle." Alexander suggests that designers should enhance our fondness for circular gatherings by creating protected, circular spaces for conversation with "each sitting space in a position...not cut by paths or movement…"

I follow these sage words whenever I can. In the photo at top, I created a small circular conversation area off a main walk. People always stop here and chat for a while, sitting on the curved low sitting wall. The circular shape makes

This spa highlights the power of the circle to draw people in. It also complements the semi-circular stone wall.

a simple, bold statement. I had a similar intention when I designed a large circular outdoor spa against a tall stone wall. The two concentric circles are a strong visual element, while the rear wall provides a feeling of sanctuary and the water enchants. These three elements – simplicity, sanctuary and delight – are what makes this outdoor setting so serene and enticing.

Circular outdoor spaces embrace us and promote conviviality. For a magnificent site that enjoyed a fabulous sunset view of the Hudson River, I designed a 16-foot-diameter round patio, partially enclosed by a low stone wall (see bottom photo). This "terrace-in-the-round" is a lovely place to enjoy a spectacular vista. I reinforced the circle shape here by defining the patio with a ribbon of bluestone pavers and stone edging.

"Squaring the Circle"

A circle is the perfect shape for an entry door landing. I installed a round, granite millstone within a "meet and greet" area by a side door (next page). Although it is not the front entrance, it is

A round patio encourages socializing.

A large, inscribed circle in a side door landing makes the area seem extra-special.

the door most people use to enter the house. By adding a circular accent, I transformed what might have been a utilitarian space into an inviting gathering spot. The inscribed sunburst pattern in the stone provides a dynamic quality to the scene.

In order to fit the circular millstone within the new bluestone paving, brick was used to "square the circle." The brick corners inserted around the stone are a strong contrast, which makes the

The circular millstone with a sunburst pattern, closeup. Note the brick that "squares the circle."

stone stand out. The brick also matches the brick cap of the wall next to the landing.

Council Rings: An American Outdoor Tradition

Nowhere is the circular shape more prized in the landscape than in the rustic council rings of author and naturalist Ernest T. Seton's Woodcraft Camps. First established in the early 20th century, the camps' central congregation areas were large circular spaces built in forest clearings, similar to the original Native American tribal council rings. The campers would sit on low split-log benches that formed the perimeter of the circle. Seton wrote in his book *The Birch Bark Roll* that the round shape of the rings called

A curved stone bench is one way to create a council ring.

up the "ancient spirit of the woods"; he felt that the circular area should never be traversed by campers except by official request.

Jens Jensen, a well-known Midwestern landscape architect of that time, admired council rings so much that he made them a signature feature in his many public parks. He called the council ring "one of the great symbols of

I designed this bench as a place to sit and enjoy the garden scene.

mankind" and believed the circular areas inspired people to "read poetry or tell stories, to act out dramas, or simply to meditate, especially on humanity's relationship with nature." (from *Jens Jensen: Maker of Natural Parks and Gardens,* by Robert E. Grese)

Following this idea, I have designed stone council rings for several woodland gardens. One particularly inviting circle, shown in photo above, is located in a hickory and maple wood and measures 20 feet in diameter. It is a stone bench formed from a 3-inch-thick curved bluestone seat

set atop three evenly spaced fieldstone piers, or legs. The bench makes up part of the ring and the remainder is defined by rocks set flush in the ground. Everyone who goes there almost always sits down to enjoy the scene.

Spirals in the Landscape

Everyone is intrigued by the spiral shape, the symbol of natural growth. Plant beds shaped as spirals are most captivating. You can make a swirling spiral pattern of compact herbs such as germander (Teuchrium chamaedrys), *thyme* (Thymus vulgaris) *or sage* (Salvia). *Low boxwood hedges and lavender also work well to define a spiral shape. I have even planted a spiral vegetable garden, which is a fun way to grow your veggies! For an extra-special, exotic effect, you can even create a spiral pattern from stones.*

Creeping thyme makes a lovely spiral plant bed.

Ovals: Classic and Serene

Ovals are elegant, elongated circles that add graciousness to a land-scape. They lend themselves to outdoor ceremonial spaces, as is clear in the U.S. national park, The Ellipse, in Washington, DC – officially called the President's Park South. This 16-acre lawn, the largest outdoor oval in the world, abuts the White House grounds and was part of the original 18th-century city plan designed by the French-born American architect and civil engineer Pierre L'Enfant. It was installed by the Army Corps of Engineers in 1877 and no one knows how they laid out this immense "flattened circle" so accurately. The Ellipse is used for large gatherings, strolling and the annual Christmas tree lighting.

This oval is a subtle way to make the level lawn more interesting.

The curved embrace of an oval shape in a land-scape invites us to enter. That is why I inserted an oval shape in a lawn for Making Headway, a foundation dedicated to children afflicted with brain and spinal cord tumors. Every year they host an outdoor party for about 300 children and their families.

In one section of their sloping property, I created a level lawn and installed a border of bluestone in the shape of an oval "racetrack" with straight sides and rounded ends. When viewed from above, this simple bounded shape nestled in a hillside is a silent invitation to come down and explore further.

Bluestone pavers fit together to create a curved line.

The Power of the Square and Rectangle in the Landscape

We instinctively enjoy sitting in a rectilinear space with 90-degree corners. The two red maple trees accentuate the angle.

We are so familiar with rectangles and their parallel sides and 90-degree corners that we hardly consider any other shape when building a house, designing a park or even laying out a vegetable garden or paved patio. Our preference for rectilinear outdoor spaces harks back to the historic town "square," which almost always was in the shape of a rectangle or square. Indeed, our urban parks, such as Central Park in New York City, the Boston Common, Golden Gate Park in San Francisco and the National Mall in Washington, DC, are, in their entirety, large rectangular shapes. Their orderliness and predictability appeal to us above all else.

You could say that in the melody of form, the stable firmness of the square and rectangle is like a soothing song that relaxes us. We feel secure in a corner and walk comfortably through a rectangular plaza.

The Lure of a Sheltered Corner
We all love to sit in a protected corner looking out to a view. This is why people seek out the proverbial "table in the corner" in a restaurant; it provides the sanctuary that I call, "the lure of a sheltered corner." If you create a rectangular patio and provide an outdoor seating area in a corner backed by bushes, a wall or a slope everyone will

The lure of a sheltered corner. Here, the 'Nikko Blue' hydrangea *(Hydrangea macrophylla* 'Nikko Blue'*)* and laceleaf hydrangea are backed by 'Allegheny' leatherleaf viburnums *(Viburnum* x *rhytidophylloides* 'Allegheny'*)*.

Golden Rectangles and the Divine Proportion

The rectangle that is the most pleasing to our eye is the "golden rectangle." It has a long side that is roughly two-thirds longer than its shorter side. In fact it is 1:1.618 longer, which is the phi ratio (Ø). Phi is the mathematical proportion we see in every natural form – in our bodies, plants, flowers, fruit and shells. It is the "universal constant of design." Our unspoken familiarity with the proportion of 1:1.618 ensures a sense of harmony in any outdoor space that contains it.

want to sit in this cozy spot! And if you provide a view of some sort then it will be even more appealing. (See photo above.)

I used colored concrete squares and rectangles to create an irregular pattern and draw the eye into this garden.

You can create a protected corner next to your house by using the rear wall as one side of the corner and a low hedge as the other side. This combination makes a wonderful niche for a small table and chairs.

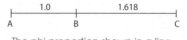

The phi proportion shown in a line.

A rectangular space using the proportions of phi just feels "right" to us. Le Corbusier, the renowned 20th-century French architect, used phi in all his creations, saying a design system using phi proportions represents, "the mathematics of the human body, gracious, elegant, and firm, the source of that harmony which moves us, beauty..."

If you look closely, you can see golden rectangles in many paintings, buildings and outdoor spaces. This shape has been utilized by artists and architects since time immemorial. The Japanese temple makers used it, as did Renaissance painters, medieval architects and several modern artists and designers. It can be found in the Greek Parthenon, in Paris's Notre Dame Cathedral and in Columbia University's Low Memorial Library in New York City. You can also find golden rectangles in paintings by Leonard da Vinci, Piet Mondrian and Georges Seurat. And it is no coincidence that you see a golden rectangle every time you use a credit card!

The Golden Rectangle in a Japanese Temple. The ancient designers of the revered Ise Shrine in Japan knew about the salutary effect of the phi ratio. This Shinto temple dates back to the 7th century and looks exactly as it did hundreds of years ago because every 20 years it is torn down and faithfully rebuilt with the same materials and techniques to preserve its historical integrity. According to architect György Doczi, the golden rectangle can be found in many parts of the shrine's design. In his book *The*

Power of Limits: Proportional Harmonies in Nature, Art, and Architecture, he writes: "The plan…is a single golden rectangle. The gable elevation, from ground to ridgeline and from eave to eave, corresponds to two golden rectangles. The side elevation…fits again two golden rectangles, topped by two larger ones that cover the roof itself. Nothing is arbitrary." Fabric designer Jack Lenor Larsen was so impressed with the Ise Shrine and its proportions that he patterned his home, LongHouse Reserve, in East Hampton, New York, on it. This beautifully landscaped property is now open to the public and is a must-see for all garden lovers.

The LongHouse Reserve in East Hampton, NY, was designed by Jack Lenor Larsen and is modeled on the ancient Ise Shrine of Japan.

Including Golden Rectangles in Your Garden. Making the rectangular spaces in your garden in the phi proportion is easy to do. You simply multiply the dimension that you want for one side of the rectangular space by 1.62 (you can round it up to 1.62 from 1.618) to find the phi length for the longer side. For example, if you want the width of the rectangle to be 14 feet wide, you then multiply 14 by 1.62 to get the approximate length of 22 feet 8 inches for the length (see figure below.) Conversely, if you know what the longer side should be, then multiply it by .618 to get the corresponding shorter width.

Another view of the golden rectangle patio.

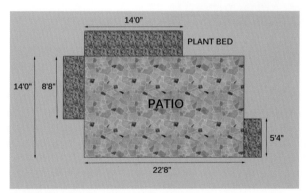

The phi proportions repeat themselves in a golden rectangle patio layout. The plant beds are in phi proportion to the patio length and width.

The Fibonacci series of numbers can help here, too. Three hundred years before Columbus, Leonardo of Pisa, better known as Fibonacci, uncovered a link merging mathematics with nature and art. He noted how fast rabbits could breed in ideal circumstances and puzzled over the offspring: how many pairs will there be in one year? This mathematical series led to a certain sequence of numbers that is now immortalized as the Fibonacci series.

Each successive number in the series is the sum of the two preceding numbers: 1+1=2, 2+1=3, 3+2=5, 5+3=8, 8+5=13, 13+8=21, 21+13=34, 34+21=55, and so on. And as the numbers climb, the ratio of the two successive numbers comes close to phi or 1.618. That is, the previous number, when multiplied by 1.618, yields the following number. This optimized system for growth is evident in many of Nature's forms - the phi proportion reveals itself in the geometric spiraling of seeds in a sunflower, the growth of a nautilus, even in pine cones and pineapples.

A rectangular entry terrace with the right proportions is very inviting.

all the features will be in phi proportion to each other. It will be a very harmonious layout to the eye.

This approach also works well for a front door landing and steps. To make them in the proportions of a golden rectangle, center 5-foot-long entry steps within an 8-foot-long paved landing. (See figure below.) These are both in the Fibonacci series, 8 being approximately 1.62 times larger than 5. It also provides for an additional 18 inches extending out on either side of the steps, which is enough for a good-sized flowerpot.

The beauty and constancy of the phi proportion becomes apparent when you lay out a patio in a golden rectangle and then use phi again to lay out the plant beds around it (see figures on preceding page). This can be the length of the plant bed that borders one side of the rectangular terrace and is in approximate phi proportion to 14 feet. Likewise, if you subtract 8 feet 8 inches from 14 feet, you get 5 feet 4 inches, which is in phi proportion to 8 feet 8 inches. By installing another plant bed of this length on the opposite side of the terrace you will have a design where

The dimensions shown here are in approximate phi proportion to each other. Phi is 1.618.

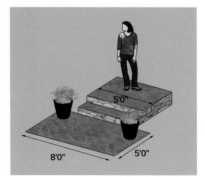

I hinted at a rectangle with this low retaining wall in a contemporary landscape.

*   *   *

Making music for the eye

Simple forms like the circle, square and oval are inherently beautiful in a garden. When you incorporate these shapes with the right proportions it creates a visual harmony that promotes relaxation and helps to slow us down. You can enhance this music for the eye with lyrical, curving walks or staccato, stepping-stone paths; with square patios – solid and comfortable, like a sonorous melody; with visually rhythmic repetitive planting patterns. There so much more, of course. It's yours to compose. 🍁

Calling on the Trees

God is the experience of looking at a tree and saying, "Ah!"
– Joseph Campbell

emember when climbing a tree was one of the most satisfying of pursuits? Sitting on a branch, with leaves rustling overhead, you felt safe looking down on the world below. Trees, as all tree-climbing children know, are our silent allies. They grow amidst the tumult of human activity; they beautify the environment, cool the air, provide food and wood and stabilize hillsides. What a gift from Nature! No wonder ancient cultures saw these largest and longest-lived plant forms as founts of wisdom, fertility and courage. Swiss psychologist C. G. Jung took it a bit further, opining in his autobiography *Memories, Dreams, Reflections* that trees are the "direct embodiments of the incomprehensible meaning of life." The presence of trees in your garden can enrich the environment in so many ways, from the practical to the mysterious. And you can call on them, just as you may have done when you were young.

May the Forest Be With You

Pre-industrial societies saw trees as being inhabited by unseen beings. The ancient Greeks believed invisible female deities, the dryads, lived within specific trees, such as oaks. When you entered an oak grove it was understood that you were crossing into the dryads' domain. The ancient Japanese also saw trees as being enlivened by female presences. One of their tales tells of a man who meets a girl under his cherished willow tree. He marries her. When the emperor orders that the willow be cut down to build a temple, the man's wife informs him that she is the spirit of the tree and dies as the tree is felled.

Hindu teachings also assert that formless spirits, known as devas, live within trees. A verse from one of these centuries-old texts, or *shastras,* tells us, "Trees serve as homes for visiting *devas,* who do not manifest in earthly bodies, but live in the fibers of the trunks and larger branches of the trees, feed from the leaves and communicate through the tree itself." Following this belief, there are sacred, native forests in India called *Devavanas,* where the cutting of trees, or even harming a branch, is forbidden.

The Celts of ancient Europe believed that Nemetona, goddess of the grove, resided in the hushed atmosphere of forest glades. She could be found in a needle-covered pine forest, beneath a group of towering beech trees or in a sun-dappled birch grove. These woodland clearings were called nemetons and were seen as being awash with the enchanted energies of trees.

Trees: Nature's Recharger

The Celts attributed the charged atmosphere of woodland clearings to *shunnache,* the life energy of trees. Interestingly, this ancient notion is similar to the invisible energy fields of modern physics, and Albert Einstein's famous equation, $E = MC^2$, that states that all matter is made up of light and energy. Perhaps the Celtic *shunnache,* the Hindu tree devas and Greek dryads are really references to Einstein's light energy, perceived or sensed by our ancestors. As the popular movie *Avatar* postulates, trees may be made up of energizing light fibers that permeate the area around it. It would seem that this force field is what uplifts us and gladdens our heart when we are in an undisturbed forest.

Tall trees border a wide walk in Lotusland, a garden in Santa Barbara, California, and provide needed shade. The trees form a majestic setting.

was aware of its skyward-reaching arms and up-turned finger-tips, as if some vivid life (or electricity) was streaming through them far into the spaces of heaven." The Chinese call this energy *chi*. In fact, feng shui practitioners use the chi of healthy trees as a visual barometer to determine propitious locations. A vigorous tree indicates a healthy area.

In Japan, the health-giving properties of trees are the basis of a popular medical therapy called "forest bathing." Japanese researchers found that when people walk slowly through a national "therapy forest," inhaling the air, their stress hormones are lowered and the activity of cancer-fighting cells is increased. Thus, Japanese doctors tell their patients to take a leisurely walk in a forest to strengthen their immune system. Dr. Roger S. Ulrich, an environmental psychologist at Texas A&M University found a similar result: within five minutes of looking at a setting containing trees, people's blood pressure dropped and their muscle tension eased. In other studies by Dr. Ulrich, this effect held true even if the test subjects were viewing videos and not the real thing. Now imagine the change in your blood pressure if, instead of just looking at trees, you were in their midst!

The historian Edward Carpenter described a certain tree energy that he encountered in early spring. He writes that one afternoon, as he passed a particular beech tree, "Suddenly I

Plant a "Cathedral of Trees"

You can create your own forest therapy park by planting several trees together in a group. This artificial grove, in time, will become like a leafy "cathedral of trees" that cools the air when it's hot and helps keep the surroundings warmer when it's cold. Trees planted close together regulate the temperature and humidity within their boundaries and offer wind and drought protection as well. I plant groups of trees in three general layouts: as a grid, a natural grove or a mounded tree grove.

A Grid Arrangement

This is an ordered layout made up of parallel rows of trees, spaced equidistantly. The straight lines of trees form an appropriate landscaped setting for a contemporary suburban home or a public outdoor space in an urban environment. The trees may be planted directly in the ground, within raised planters or surrounded by paving, loose gravel or low-growing plants.

Dan Kiley, a landscape architect, became famous for these geometric "bosques," as he called them. In Burlington, Vermont, Kiley planted a grid of 123 locust trees around the modern Cathedral of the Immaculate Conception. The precise arrangement of the trees provides a visual rhythm to the surroundings and an enticing, shady atmosphere to all who enter.

A Natural Grove

As its name suggests, this grove follows nature's example and is the opposite of the grid. Here,

An evenly spaced grid of plane trees *(Platanus acerifolia).* In summer these trees create a leafy and shady canopy.

naturally. Similarly, a grouping of larch trees *(Larix decidua),* the native deciduous conifer, (see left) or columnar sweetgum trees *(Liquidambar styriciflua* 'Slender Silhouette') (see photo, right) in a far off corner makes an alluring destination. You

Tall columnar trees like these 'Slender Silhouette' sweetgums are striking for the height, shape and fall color.

The deciduous conifer, the larch, grows naturally in groves. This planting of several larches recreates a grove at the Steinhardt garden.

can plant trees along both sides of a garden path to make it feel like a sheltered corridor.

I once planted a grove of 'Whitespire' birch trees *(Betula populifolia* 'Whitespire') on a hillside that had been denuded by a developer. I first placed a row of dark-green Norway spruce *(Picea abies)* and located the white-barked birch trees in front them. Evergreen trees such as spruce, cedar and pine make a beautiful and protective windbreak for more delicate trees such as birch. Today, the straight white trunks of the 'Whitespire' birch are quite striking against the tall, evergreen backdrop.

trees are planted together as they might normally occur – by rock outcrops, on sheltered hillsides or at the edge of woods. For example, a cluster of white flowering dogwoods *(Cornus florida)* on a hillside is captivating and looks as if it happened

A grove of trees on a mound is striking silhouetted against the open sky, as shown here at Storm King Art Center in Mountainville, NY.

A Mounded Tree Grove

This grouping is my favorite type of layout for trees in a garden. It recreates the natural tendency of certain trees to grow together on a mound, such as shown in the photo of a Richard Serra sculpture and nearby trees at Storm King Art Center in Mountainville, New York.

This technique requires that you create a low mound and plant a group of trees in a staggered pattern (the spacing depends on the tree species) atop it. The mound should be at least 20 inches high at its apex, if not more. The trees highlight the topography. For added interest, you can space the trees unequally and set large rocks within the mound or along its edge. Tall, narrow, columnar trees such as fastigiate European beech *(Carpinus betulus* 'Fastigiata'*)* or wide, low-growing ones such as witchhazel *(Hamamelis* spp.*)* or Japanese maple *(Acer palmatum)* look beautiful growing on mounds.

Special Trees for Grove Plantings

A grove of trees not only provides interest in bark texture, fall leaf color and growth habit, but also provides habitat for birds and small mammals. Some trees do especially well planted close together, probably because they prefer to grow this way in their native habitat. Here are three tree species that are suitable for a grove planting.

Japanese Cedar

The evergreen Japanese cedar *(Cryptomeria japonica)* is the beloved national tree of Japan, known as Sugi. It is well suited for a grove and grows to an impressive size. This deep-green tree, kin to the redwood and not a true cedar, instills a calming presence in a garden, perhaps due to its delicate but energizing cedar-like fragrance.

The Japanese revere this tree. There is an interesting piece of history around a group of of Japan's most famous Sugi trees. It goes back to the early 1600s. In his book *The Forest Flora of Japan: Garden and Forest,* Charles Sprague Sargent recounts the story of a poor vassal of the recently deceased shogun Tokugawa Ieyasu. The vassal was unable to contribute anything of appropriate value to the shogun's shrine in Nikko, which vexed him greatly. He then had an idea: he asked permission to plant young Sugi trees along an avenue leading to the site so that "future visitors might be protected from the heat of the sun." Many of these trees still survive. Today, a double row of tall *Cryptomerias* lines the road to Nikko – for forty miles.

The stateliness of Japanese cedars makes them elegant candidates for a grove planting. Since they grow relatively fast, you can plant young trees, knowing they will quickly attain sizeable proportions. However, there are smaller growing varieties of *Cryptomeria* that lend themselves to smaller gardens. One variety I like is 'Black Dragon'. It is dark green and grows about 15 feet tall. It develops a lovely pyramidal shape and suffuses the air with a fresh evergreen fragrance. You

Smaller statured 'Black Dragon' *Cryptomeria* trees look great in a grouping. I planted these to screen some steps.

can plant three 'Black Dragon' *Cryptomerias* on a mound amidst other low-growing shrubs for a stunning effect.

White Birch

White birch trees naturally grow in groups in a forest habitat and benefit from the protective microclimate there. A group of white-barked birch trees is lovely in all seasons. In spring, their catkins hang

White paper-bark birch trees *(Betula papyrifera)* grow naturally in a group.

gracefully from budding branches; in summer, the white trunks stand out against verdant foliage, and in fall, the yellow leaves seem to glow. When growing birches in a group, you can selectively prune the lower branches to create a higher canopy.

There are several white birch varieties you can use in a grove, including multi-stem or single trunk varieties. These include the native paper birch *(Betula papyrifera),* the smaller but faster growing gray birch *(B. populifolia)* and its variety 'Whitespire', or the striking Himalayan white birch *(B. utilis 'Jacquemonti').*

Plane Tree

The American sycamore *(Platanus occidentalis),* the Western sycamore *(Platanus racemosa)* and a modern cousin, the London plane *(Platanus x acerifolia),* are all wonderful candidates for planting in a group in a large space. Their mottled trunks of brown, green, gray, and white bark in a "camouflage" pattern are a striking addition in any landscape. At the Pepsico headquarters in Purchase, New York, a large grid of London plane trees, trimmed neatly, provides shade for both employees and visitors in an outdoor seating area adjacent to the cafeteria. The tree can be easily identified by its hanging pom-pom fruits in winter. Hardy and resilient, it thrives even in cramped spaces.

The London plane tree is known for its distinctive 'camouflage' bark.

In New York City, London plane trees are so predominant that their distinctive leaf is the logo of the New York Parks Department.

Calling on the Trees

A resilient tree offers us silent support. This tree, growing out of a rock, speaks to us of adapting to our circumstances.

Many cultures assert that the presence of trees can lighten our mood, strengthen our resolve and even deepen our intuition! The sacred Hindu text, the *Srimad Bhagavatam,* tells us that trees are "like noble, highly elevated charitable men who never deny charity to anyone who approaches them." Indeed, there is nothing more heartening than being in the company of a great, old tree. These resilient and weathered beings offer us a kind of silent support. Zen master T. D. Suzuki acknowledged this power when he wrote in *Zen and Japanese Culture,* "Every old tree of any sort inspires a beholder with a mystic feeling which leads him to a faraway world of timeless eternity."

Reclaim the Ancient Tradition of Tree Wrapping

You can celebrate venerable trees through the ancient custom I call "tree wrapping." I use this phrase to describe the tradition that highlights certain trees as something to be protected by the community. Wrapping tree trunks or adorning branches of special trees with fiber rope, natural ribbon or fabric has been practiced for thousands of years and is a wonderful way to honor a tree.

In Japan, tree wrapping has been elevated to an art form. It derives from the Shinto belief that all natural forms are imbued with spirit. They encircle tree trunks with a braided rope called a *shimenawa.* The twisted, bulky cord is made from rice straw and holds white, zigzag paper streamers called *shide,* which act as protectors of the tree's spirit. Mythologist Joseph Campbell, in his book *Hero with a Thousand Faces,* refers to Japanese tree wrapping as "one of the most conspicuous, important and silently eloquent of the traditional symbols." In a fitting gesture, each New Year, all the *shimenawa* are removed from the trees and burned on a community bonfire. They are then replaced with new ones for another year of protection. What a memorable New Year's tradition!

The festive European "Maypole dance" is also a form of tree wrapping. This annual community celebration takes place at the most fruitful time of year, in spring or summer. The Maypole dance of Sweden takes place at the summer solstice. A pole, usually taken from a hawthorn, maple or birch tree, is decorated with green leaves and branches to simulate a tree. Several long, colored ribbons are suspended from the top of the pole

The Wishing Tree in Berkshire Botanical Garden, Stockbridge, MA.

A lovely wish on the wishing tree – The Berkshire Botanical Garden.

by Russian peasants who left them to the Mother Goddess, who was associated with the birch. A variation of this tradition is also practiced in India where local villagers pay tribute to the Hindu goddess Devi, the female aspect of the Divine, by adorning tree branches in her sacred grove.

Tree wrapping is a lovely way to remind others of the "call of the trees." Community and botanical gardens can incorporate this as a wonderful group activity and modify it as they wish. The Berkshire Botanical Garden in Stockbridge, Massachusetts, has a "Wishing Tree" where people can write messages on cards and tie them to the branches. The sign next to it describes the tradition's origins, "The Wishing Tree is a Buddhist tradition found in Asian countries. It is believed that if you put your wish on a piece of paper and tie it to the tree, the wind will blow the words into the air and your wish will come true." When we tie fabric or cards to the branches or trunks of beloved trees, we are reaffirming the irrevocable partnership between people and these wonderful plant forms. It reminds us how intertwined we are and that what we save, saves us.

and the celebrants, each holding the end of a ribbon, weave in and around each other until the ribbons are woven together around the "tree," meeting at the base.

It is believed that the Maypole celebration came from the Siberian custom of tying narrow fabric bands or ceremonial silk scarves to the branches of an especially vigorous tree. This tree serves as an intermediary with the invisible world. Each fabric tie transmits prayers for personal and world peace. Up through the 19th century, "ritual towels" were hung on the branches of birch trees

Wendell Berry, the great nature writer, once said in an NPR radio interview, "You've got to understand what kind of creature a tree is… they have to receive from us certain deference, a certain respect, as we would extend to any neighbor."

When we connect with our "neighbor" trees on a subtle level, we may be surprised to find that they respond! Like the adage that recommends you "talk to your plants," any kind of communication with a tree is rewarded. Walt Whitman noted this in his poem "Song of the Open Road," when he asked, "Why are there trees I never walk under but large and melodious thoughts descend upon me? (I think they hang there winter and summer on those trees, and always drop fruit as I pass;)" The bestowal of such thoughts is, as Whitman opined, a tree's great gift to us.

To attune to a tree all you have to do is simply touch it. The act of placing both hands on a tree is very empowering. Martha Beck, the author of *Expecting Adam: A True Story of Birth, Rebirth, and Everyday Magic,* tells of a memorable encounter with a tree: "I walked up to one tree and put my hands against its bark, congratulating it on its courage, trying to draw on its strength. The tree was warm under my hands. I swear I felt it communicating back to me, with its own brand of comfort and compassion." Trees support us, in their own arboreal way.

If you have a particular tree you feel drawn to, sit comfortably at its base (you can bring a pillow or mat) and rest against its trunk. You can also face it, touching the bark lightly with your hands. Relax, breathe deeply, and let go of your thoughts as best you can, so there is an opening for an image, thought or feeling to form. Ask

Trees, such as this oak, can be our silent allies.

silently for the tree's aid. At first, all you may experience is a vague feeling or a deep silence. A tree may appear to be slow to respond, but as you strengthen your receptive abilities in this new way of communicating you will feel its energy. Repeated visits to the same tree produce a clearer response. Even if you think nothing has transpired, please know that trees do not communicate on a mental level and that your invitation to a tree never goes unheeded. This quiet act energizes both you and the tree in a subtle way. Always thank a tree (silently or aloud) when you depart.

Once you commune with a tree you may feel how each species of tree affects us differently. Tradition tells us that pines, poplars and birch trees pacify us and remove stress. Oaks help to anchor and steady us. Sandalwood trees enhance our awareness. As Thomas Hardy wrote in *Under the Greenwood Tree,* "To dwellers in a wood, almost every species of tree has its voice as well as its feature."

The apple tree, for example, is universally acknowledged in mythology and folklore as an emblem of fruitfulness, youth and love. In Germany, it was customary to plant an apple tree for every boy that was born (and a pear for each girl). The fruit trees gave strength to the marriage and the children.

The oak tree is known as the king of the forest and has long been a symbol of endurance and courage. It adds an indomitable spirit to any landscape. There are varieties of oak trees for all climatic regions; in fact, there are more than 60 species of oak growing in the United States alone. This long-lived tree was voted the people's choice in 2004 as "America's National Tree." And in 2012 more than 400 swamp white oak trees *(Quercus bicolor)* were planted at the World Trade Center Memorial in New York City.

The eastern white pine of North America *(Pinus strobus)* bestows peace on its surroundings. It exhorts us to seek serenity above all. Its power can be felt coming from the tips of its needles in the summer. The peaceful aspects of this tree are reflected in a true story about a time, several centuries ago, when the leader of the Five Nations of the Iroquois League instructed the tribes located in modern-day New York State to bury their weapons in the shade of a towering white pine tree. The leader was called the Peacemaker and he proclaimed, "If any man or nation shows a desire to obey the Great Law of Peace, they may trace the Roots to their source... and be welcomed to take shelter beneath the Tree." Thus it is that the white pine became known as the Iroquois "Tree of Peace."

Trees that Speak to Us

Drawing from Native American, Celtic and other sources of tree lore, I have compiled a list of the essential qualities of sixteen familiar trees. There are trees that build your self-confidence, help lighten your spirit or inspire you artistically. The list below can help you choose a tree whose traits you would like to invite into your garden. You can discern for yourself what virtues and benefits a specific tree holds just by being in its presence.

Apple tree

Apple. Protection, facilitates good will, promotes harmony

Ash. Grounding, aids positive outlook, increases perception

Aspen. Protection, helps to calm, overcomes fear of unknown

Beech. Prosperity, tree of learning, promotes tolerance and inner strength

Birch. Resilience, unselfishness, renewal, health, wisdom

Cedar. Purification, banishes negativity, tree of good fortune, incorruptibility

Hawthorn. Proper alignment, helps being in the present

Hazel. Tree of teaching and knowledge, inspires creative endeavors, healing

Hickory. Encourages discipline, balance and flexibility

Beech tree

Birch tree

Magnolia tree

Pine. Broadens perspective, aids in problem solving, uplifting

Spruce. Encourages wellbeing

Sycamore. Aids communication, love, offers vitality

Willow. Assists healing, eases sadness, affirms intuition

Pine tree

Maple tree

Magnolia. Enhances clarity, love, self-awareness

Maple. Prosperity, engenders good will, neutralizes negativity

Oak. Promotes endurance, power to prevail, bravery

Spruce tree

Small Trees to Enchant a Garden

Kwanzan cherry trees *(Prunus serrulata* 'Kwanzan') frame a vista.

Japanese flowering cherry trees are known for their exuberant spring blossoms. But the wide-spreading canopy of the cherry tree is also excellent for framing a scene. You can lightly prune its branches to compose a picture in your garden that looks much like a Japanese woodblock print. I did this in the scene shown in the photo at left. Two existing Kwanzan cherry trees *(Prunus serrulata* 'Kwanzan') were at the end of a dramatic long view, but they were overgrown and neglected, so I pruned their branches to frame the vista of the house and lawn. The result is a verdant foreground that entices one onward into the space. Other ornamental trees that can be used to frame a scene like this include eastern redbud *(Cercis canadensis),* Japanese Yoshino cherry *(Prunus* x *yedoensis* 'Akebono') and flowering dogwood *(Cornus florida).*

While grand old trees thrill us, it is the smaller ornamental trees that unify a garden. They strike a visual balance between their taller cousins and shorter shrubs and provide unparalleled seasonal interest in a landscape. Small-statured trees such as Japanese maple, dogwood and crabapple often sport a vivid display of flowers, fruit and/ or fall color, or provide a beautiful branching habit. They are lovely when bordering a walk or drive, framing a view or acting as a sculptural focal point.

The maroon, lacy leaves of the threadleaf Japanese maple hang delicately over a stone wall, enveloping a happy looking Buddha.

Following are some wonderful small trees that you may use to enchant a garden. They all withstand adverse conditions, are fairly free of problems, and provide color or interest in the form of abundant blossoms, fruit or colorful leaves. Since many small trees are "understory" trees that naturally grow beneath the higher canopies of taller trees, they will do well in light, dappled shade.

Threadleaf Japanese maple *(Acer palmatum dissectum)* and its many varieties are among my favorite small trees. Their wide-spreading, low-branching shape features lacy, deep-cut leaves that form a delicate weeping effect. They look especially graceful cascading over a large rock or beside a pool or stream. The variety 'Crimson

Queen' holds its deep burgundy color throughout summer and fall and looks stunning against larger-leaved green plants such as hollies, rhododendrons, and mountain laurel.

Golden full moon maple *(Acer shirasawanum* 'Aureum'*)* is another special Japanese maple. This slow-growing tree grows no higher than 25 feet and has beautiful yellow-green foliage and prominent red seeds that make it a showpiece in the landscape. It attains quite a stately character as it ages.

The golden full moon Japanese maple *(Acer shirasawanum* 'Aureum'*)* is slow growing and relatively hardy and it slowly develops into a showpiece in the garden. This tree is at the Steinhardt garden in Bedford, NY.

Kousa dogwood (*Cornus* var. *kousa*) is a small-growing tree that dazzles with its white flowers in midsummer. It spreads out as wide as it is tall and can reach up to 25 feet. The kousa dogwood has bark that develops a mottled appearance, revealing a mix of gray, tan and mahogany-brown. The fruit of the tree looks somewhat like large raspberries, appearing from late August through October.

The Kousa dogwood's fruit looks like large raspberries.

The beautiful white flowers of the Kousa dogwood.

One of my favorite cultivars is 'Milky Way', which has so many white flowers that they can conceal the foliage. In the garden shown here, I planted a Kousa dogwood on a hill to catch the eye from afar.

Willow-leaved pear *(Pyrus salicifolia* 'Pendula') is a refined small-statured, weeping tree. Its serene quality is enhanced by its dainty silvery leaves and creamy white flowers in spring. The

The 'Silver Frost' willow-leaved pear tree adds a sense of refinement to a scene.

The Kousa dogwood is covered in white flowers in later spring and early summer. I planted this tree when it was small and it has grown into a magnificent specimen!

Some crabapple trees feed the birds in fall with their fruit.

variety, 'Silver Frost', grows to only 15 feet and has cascading foliage that lights up any corner. It is a wonderful specimen tree for planters, in small urban gardens and for bordering a walk. In this scene at the New York Botanical Garden, the pear tree sets off a bench sweetly (photo on page 59, bottom right).

Crabapple (*Malus* var.) is the star of the springtime with its abundant flower display! These blooming performers grab the eye with flowers that can range from white to pink to reddish purple. Some varieties have leaves that turn from dark green to burgundy, while others have brightly colored fruit that birds love to eat. Crabapple trees look adorned with jewelry in the fall, as shown in photo at left.

Shadbush or serviceberry *(Amelanchier* var.*)* is an early-spring flowering arboreal treasure that dots the edges of woodlands with its white blooms. Shadbush offers year-round interest with fleecy white flowers followed by small berries in June and a combination of orange, purple and red leaves in autumn.

A plum tree can be trained against a wall as shown here.

Shadbush or serviceberry flowers early and sports colorful berries in June.

Many fruit trees can be trained as an "espalier" to grow against a stone wall or lattice fence. In the photo above, a plum tree, rigorously pruned for years, exhibits its luscious purple fruit like ovoid jewels against a wall.

*   *   *

There is so much more to discover and understand about these wondrous beings in our midst that we call trees. I hope this chapter will inspire you to call on their great generosity and invite them into your garden. 🍃

FOUR

The Magic of Water

If there is magic on this planet, it is contained in water.
— Loren Eiseley

Water is the magical ingredient in a garden. It catches the light in languid pools and rocky cascades. It scintillates and delights, infusing the atmosphere with an ethereal mist. The serene appeal of water lies in its never-ending ability to refresh our spirits. We are as water lilies floating atop a spring-fed pond, constantly renewed by water's life-giving properties.

In times past, cascades were believed to be inhabited by friendly, female water spirits. This cascade is in the New York Botanical Garden rock garden.

helpers, replenishing our energy and tending to plants and flowers. Of course, attributing human form and characteristics to a nonhuman thing may seem like fanciful thinking, but, as with tree devas, the undines may be an anthropomorphic description of nonvisible quantum forces in nature. You can almost feel these "nymph-like" energies when you sit by a stream or gaze upon a pond.

One compelling way to incorporate the magic of water in a garden is to have it trickle out from a rock cleft or from between two rocks set close together. The thin line of water dances and sparkles as it runs along, enticing us to reach out and touch it. If you place this trickling water in a lightly shaded niche and set a bench nearby, people will most certainly stop and enjoy a sweet moment of respite.

Water trickling out of a rock cleft in the Japanese garden of Huntington Botanical Gardens in San Marino, California is a wonderful surprise next to a stairway.

In times past, waterfalls, mountain springs and streams were believed to be inhabited by friendly female water spirits. These diminutive beings were referred to as *undines* by the medieval European alchemist Paracelsus. Like the Indian devas of the trees, undines were thought to be

The Waters of Innisfree

Some of my favorite water features can be found in the remarkable landscape known as Innisfree, in Millbrook, New York. This 185-acre naturalistic haven was created about 80 years ago by the late Walter Beck, an American painter who was inspired by the work of the 8th-century Chinese artist Wang Wei. The scholarly Beck, described as a "mystical man," spent more than 20 years moving rocks and soil to create his individual "teacup" gardens in accordance with the lay of the land. After his death, his close collaborator, the landscape architect Lester Collins, continued the task and spent 40 years refining the grounds to become the masterpiece it is today. Mr. Collins wrote that the garden "requires a stroll over serpentine, seemingly aimless garden arteries. The observer walks into a series of episodes, like Alice through the looking glass." Today, Innisfree is open to the public from May through October.

Beck and Collins were both enamored with water and its various forms. They meticulously designed springs, waterfalls and streams, and placed them all over the grounds. Thus, the sound of dripping, misting, splashing or rushing water is a constant companion as you walk through this outdoor haven. The water's movement is due to the large natural lake within Innisfree, called Tyrrel Lake. Beck used the lake as a water source and pumped the water up to a hilltop reservoir. This gravity-fed water system feeds all the streams, waterfalls and fountains and, unbelievably, is still working today.

Walter Beck's adeptness in working with stone and water in the landscape may have come from his experience as a painter. He described his approach in his book *Painting with Starch:* "One does

Innisfree's water features such as this aptly named "Hillside Cave," delight and intrigue visitors.

not think in dimensions or of restrictions; one is swayed by rhythms, and there is a willingness to follow wherever the experiment leads." This approach was also followed by Collins, who created the mysterious water feature "Hillside Cave," which provides endless enchantment as water burbles out of a magnificent ferny rock outcrop. It drips on an irregular series of rocky ledges and collects in a deep pool, where it travels back down into the earth.

The sounds of this naturalistic dripping spring are varied and delightful. Beck was very particular about the sounds of water and so he used a combination of native granite, sandstone, quartz, and limestone from the property in his creations to create a symphony of tones.

Water is everywhere at Innisfree. As you wander the grounds, you will find a "mist fountain" that disperses clouds of water vapor from atop a high rocky outcrop; a sinuous stream that travels through ferns, primroses, and sedge; a geyser-like fountain jet within a pine forest on an island; and modern structural water fountain near a brick terrace.

You can go to this delightful woodland garden and see the shared vision of Lester Collins and Walter Beck in person. Innisfree has opened its gates to visitors from around the world since 1960. Please go to www.innisfreegarden.org for more information.

The many water features of Innisfree, a public garden in Millbrook, NY, run by the Innisfree Foundation.

Create Your Own Bubbling Spring

The playful excitement of spouting water or a glimmering trickle enchants any space. Even if you don't have the force of water flowing down from a high reservoir as they do in Innisfree, you can use a small submersible pump to recirculate the water. First determine where your bubbling spring might be placed – consider putting it in an overlooked corner, next to a wall or along a shady walk. A small fountain or spray will highlight any niche and draw attention to it. This kind of discovery creates those sweet "aha" moments in a garden.

Mastering the art of recirculating water is not difficult. You need a rubber pond liner to create a watertight basin in the ground or you can use a plastic container to store the water underground. You also must have an underwater pump, an electrical source to power it, some flexible tubing, and a spout. The size and kind of submersible pump you choose will determine if your spring will trickle out of the earth or spray high into the air. Many garden centers offer a selection of pumps to choose from.

Moving Water: Lessons from a Paradise Garden

The ancient Persians were famous for their lavish, walled-in "paradise" gardens that featured flowing waterways and dappled shade. These verdant settings were insulated from the harsh desert winds and visitors would sit on woven carpets, enjoying the scenery, eating from the fruit trees irrigated by the canals, and inhaling the intoxicating scent of roses and jasmines. Heaven in a garden indeed! Interestingly, the word *paradise* comes from the Persian word *pairi-daeza* meaning "enclosed space."

A "quadripartite" layout of an ancient Persian garden. The central fountain feeds water into four straight channels, following the compass directions.

It makes sense that water, a treasured commodity in an arid land, would be the focus of a Persian garden. Here, water, piped in from far-off mountains, flowed continuously from a central raised fountain toward the four cardinal directions in straight, tiled channels. Paved walks paralleled the canals and were shaded by perfectly aligned sycamore, date or cypress trees. The origin of this rectilinear plan, offering tranquility within its ordered layout, comes from the garden of the Persian gardener-king Cyrus, who was called the "King of the Four Quarters."

Moving water and its salutary effect was at the heart of paradise gardens. Bubbling water would shoot into the air before travelling down the channels. But what explains the salutary effect? Today, we know that fountains, with their splashing movement, cause water molecules to break apart, permeating the air with negatively charged ions. All fountains create these invisible particles which, when inhaled, affect the levels of serotonin, or the "happy" neurotransmitter, in our brains. Negatively charged air from splashing water makes us more cheerful and helps us to relax! That is why so many of us feel compelled to sing in the shower, and why so many good ideas come to us there. It also accounts for the happy feeling we all experience at the ocean shore. How can negative ions create such positive effects? These molecules, with their extra electron, increase the production of serotonin in our bodies, causing us to experience lower stress, reduced fatigue and less anxiety. Fountains, therefore, are not only beautiful and cooling, but are nonstop mood enhancers.

Perhaps the large fountains we see in so many cities with water gushing high in the air are there to make us more content. The Trevi Fountain in Rome, the Swann Fountain in Philadelphia and the Columbus Circle fountain in New York, among many others, may make urban residents a little jollier with their splashing waters.

A Mist Fountain

Tanner Fountain, located on the campus of Harvard University in Boston, is an example of an intriguing mist fountain that give pleasure and cools. Designed by the contemporary American

Students love to lounge in the summer by the cooling Tanner Fountain, Harvard University, by Peter Walker

landscape architect, Peter Walker, it consists of a series of concentric circles of granite boulders, extending out to 60 feet in diameter. Set within the 159 boulders are 32 jets of water that spout out from the ground, creating a mist that produces rainbows in warm months. The mist descends upon the people who sit on the rocks or play in the soft sprays of water. The natural boulders add an earthy authenticity that contrasts wonderfully with the gossamer atmosphere. Misting fountains are an idea that can be replicated with easily available fog generators in any garden.

Cascades and Traveling Streams

Garden bridges offer what I call the "in-between" experience. People instinctively stop right in the middle of this bridge and look down the length of the stream.

Streams and small cascades often are centerpieces of a serene garden. The sound of water tripping over rocks and the sparkle of the sun off a moving eddy calms us and makes us a little more contemplative. Ralph Waldo Emerson describes this in his book *Nature:* "Who looks upon a river in a meditative hour, and is not reminded of the flux of all things?"

To enhance this magical effect, I doubled the drama in one landscape and created both a waterfall and a separate cascading stream that merge in a small frog pond. The waterfall is a steep, narrow drop, while the stream is a wider, somewhat languorous affair that curves through a rocky landscape and glides over smooth, rounded stones (see photos left and below). What you can't see is that the waterfall and the stream both recirculate, and the water is pumped back uphill through hidden pipes.

The plants in this cascade garden

A double cascade multiplies water's magic in this garden I designed. The large, dark green boxwood in the background anchors the scene.

include Japanese garden juniper *(Juniperus procumbens* 'Nana'), which drapes over the edges of the stream to create a beguiling effect, and a green threadleaf Japanese maple *(Acer palmatum dissectum)* hanging delicately over the pond. An arched, Japanese-style bridge (shown on the previous page) crosses the stream and offers visitors a view of the length of the watercourse.

A recirculating stream in a garden does not have to be large in order to be can be eye catching. In the New York Botanical Garden there is a very narrow stream that is almost obscured by the lovely flowers planted along its banks. It is the combination of the flowing water and the dainty pink anemones that is so enchanting here.

Stepped rocks create a syncopated water flow in this cascade.

Rounded stones along a very narrow stream look wonderful with the pink Japanese wind anemones. The word anemone is derived from the Greek word meaning "daughter of the wind" but the perennial anemone should be in a sheltered location.

The waterfall shown above right has a series of stepped rocks set within the hillside. The water ripples down this cataract in intervals. I intentionally curved the waterfall so that the top is just out of sight. Each rocky step is of varying depths to create a syncopated rhythm of water because the sound of a cascade is as important as how it looks.

Design Tips for a Superior Cascade

A small watercourse in a garden can be a metaphor for dealing with life's obstacles. It shows us how to be like moving water, flowing around obstacles in our life path. With that in mind, here are a few tips for designing a superior cascade:

- A backyard waterfall is more interesting when only a part of it is visible from the house. A half-hidden water feature creates depth and intrigue and invariably draws visitors to it. There are several ways to partially obscure a waterfall:
  1. Build it at an angle to the viewer so that a full view is impossible.
  2. Plant a large shrub in front at one side.
  3. Create a small mound to partially screen the cascade.
- In one garden, I used all three techniques. I built the cascade at a diagonal to the house, planted low plants along its rocky banks to screen a portion from view, and mounded the garden beds a little higher than the cascade so that they acted as a visual barrier.
- A waterfall can seem farther away if the top of it is higher than the viewer's eyes. In one garden, I elevated the top of the waterfall 6 feet higher than a viewer's average height and narrowed the source of the water at the

Water flowing over smoothed stones generates a certain kind of calmness.

top, which made the cascade look as if it were in the distance.
- Introduce zigzag turns in the cascade journey. This alters spatial perception and makes it more interesting.

A Waterfall's Song

The "heavenly waterfall" at the Portland Japanese Garden utilizes several design techniques that make it so captivating.

The waterfall at the Portland Japanese Garden is a striking example of these design techniques. The "heavenly waterfall," as it is called, was created by Professor Takuma Tono in 1967. The falls are partially obscured by a tree and a large shrub. The flow of water alternates between flowing left and then right, and the top of the falls is high above the line of sight.

The "heavenly waterfall" contains an example of another Japanese garden technique known as the "water-dividing stone." This entails the placement of a smaller stone directly at the base of a cascade. Water flowing down the falls breaks as it hits this submerged stone and creates a small center of splashing. The prominent "splash break" forms a visual base to the downward force of the cascade and also helps create the all-important negative ions and can alter the sound of the water as it falls.

A lovely story about this is in the Portland Japanese Garden's website, telling of a visitor's student trip there while the "heavenly waterfall" was being constructed: "The large stones had been placed and the falls were running. Professor Tono was focused on setting "one-man" stones in the waterfall's course. After several were carefully positioned in the flowing water, he walked to our side of the lower pond. With back to the falls and head bowed, he closed his eyes. After a short pause, he approached our class for discussion of what we had observed. "Were you meditating just now?" a student asked. The depth of his simple answer surprised and delighted me. "No, I was listening to the waterfall, so I might tune the harmony of its song."

Create a Dew Garden

If you take a walk early on a sunny spring morning, when the air is crisp, you may notice beads of water glistening atop the blades of grass and flowers. Like magic, these water drops of dew come out of thin air to make everything sparkle in the morning sun. And just as fast they vanish, evaporating in the warmth of the day;

the fleeting watery celebration is over.

Dew appears when the days are warm and nights are cool. In the chill night air, drops of water condense from the atmosphere and settle on whatever is near the ground. The condensation of water from the night air is so reliable that the ancient Romans used dew as a water source in the desert. They would leave sheepskins out overnight and in the morning would wring a bowl of dew water from each.

Drops of dew collect on the blossoms of spring, such as daffo-dils, pansies, clover, dianthus, phlox and

Here are dianthus blossoms after the dew dries off.

euphorbia. They glitter in the morning with tiny globes of water perched lightly upon their petals. One of the best dew catchers is the perennial flowering plant called Lady's Mantle *(Alchemilla*

The crinkled leaves of the Lady's Mantle are well known as "dew catchers."

mollis). Its botanical genus name, *Alchemilla,* is Arabic for "little magical one," which refers to the subtle properties of the dew water that collects on its wide, crinkled leaves. The dew that *Alchemilla* collects looks like clear diamond drops, giving it its other name, Dew Cup.

The therapeutic properties of dew have been known throughout history and were reaffirmed in the 1930s by Dr. Edward Bach, an English physician. He surmised that dew sitting upon a blossom absorbs the healing energies of that flower and reasoned that ingesting a small amount of a flower's sun-drenched dewdrops can balance the emotional energy patterns that lie behind many people's illnesses. Dr. Bach eventually modified the task of collecting dew by floating fresh flowers on spring water in sunlight and extracting their healing energies in this fashion. This became the famed Bach flower remedies.

Bach firmly believed that the flower essences in the water were a gift from nature. "Once we have been given a jewel of such magnitude," Bach said, "nothing can deviate us from our path of love and duty to displaying its luster, pure and unadorned to the people of the world." Who could imagine that dewdrops were nature's little healing crystal balls, magnifying and absorbing early morning sunlight? This is indeed the "magic of dew."

Knock Out® roses are consistent bloomers. In the early morning the multitude of blossoms may be covered in dew.

A Dewdrop Garden of Roses

A dewdrop garden of roses is a heavenly setting, if even for a short interlude. The sunlight is gleaming, the air refreshing, and the birdsong resounding. Dew, nature's ephemeral wonder, alights upon roses in the morning like tiny diamonds. Roses are the most beautiful dew catchers in the plant world. Nothing matches the delicacy of a tight rosebud adorned with small beads of water sparkling like jewels. As the petals unfurl, they are exquisitely traced with minute dewdrops. Roses and dew create nature's most redolent jewelry.

Roses, by the way, are morning risers and enjoy the "jump start" that dawning light provides. They grow best in soft morning sun which also dries off the dewy moisture from their foliage early in the day. For this reason, a dewdrop garden of roses will thrive in a site that faces northeast or east, home of the morning sun.

There are a host of new varieties of hardy shrub roses that you can choose from for this garden. In the category of no-fuss roses, I like the ever-blooming Knock Out® family of roses. They do not have the fragrance of other varieties, but they are disease resistant and require a minimum of care. They grow to about 4 feet tall, thus bringing the flowers closer to the eye, which makes it easier to see the dewdrops in detail.

The Splendor of Still Water

A still expanse of water is the show in this landscape. This is part of the Steinhardt Garden in Bedford, NY. You can visit here as part of the Garden Conservancy's Open days program.

The surface glassiness of still water gives us a quietness that nothing else can. Henry David Thoreau wrote of this natural mirror in his book Walden: "A lake is earth's eye; looking into which the beholder measures the depth of his own nature." Besides reflecting light, a flat expanse of water adds a deep dimension to the surroundings. It is for this reason that large pools of clear water have been central elements in the grandest landscapes since ancient times. The undisturbed lakes of the royal gardens of Versailles in France and the reflecting pool of the Taj Mahal in India echo the glory of their surroundings with shimmering color and light.

The placid pools of old are the genesis for our modern rectangular swimming pool – which can be just as inspiring if you lay it out knowledgeably. Here are a few pointers for siting a pool or pond in a landscape.

First, consider placing the approach to the pool area on a diagonal to give visitors a fuller view of the space. This "kitty-corner" approach is the opposite of a direct, straight-line entry that channels your view down the length of the pool. While this head-on view is dramatic, I find an entrance on the diagonal to be more inviting.

Second, provide enough level room around a pool to accommodate all those who want to sit

Approaching a pool area at a diagonal, as I designed here, provides depth to the view. This kind of view was preferred by the impressionist artists, as well.

difference that just a few steps can make is remarkable. It creates a separate outdoor room, providing our cherished "sanctuary." I often make a small "foyer" at the top of the steps to enhance the sense of anticipation. This stopping point is a perfect spot for a gate or bench.

The lily pond at Pepsico world headquarters in Purchase, NY, designed by Russell Page. The angled view is just as nice as the straight-on view that you experience when crossing it.

there. Often, the sitting area around a pool is tight and cramped because we all tend to focus on the water and forget about the land around it. In truth, we actually spend more time next to water than within it. My rule of thumb is to provide a level area equal to 1½ times the square footage of the pool. This sitting area can be paved with stone, brick, concrete or tile, or it can be an expanse of lawn; the only requirement is that it be fairly level.

Lastly, site your pool or pond a few steps lower or higher than the surrounding area. The

A few steps down (or up) creates a separate outdoor room. On the right of the steps, I planted Prague viburnum (*Viburnum* 'Pragense') and pruned it into a hedge to act as a dense screen.

A Reflecting Pool for Your Garden

Reflecting pools are designed for serenity. The still water acts as a mirror, bouncing light off of it. To increase a pool's reflectivity, it should have a shallow, dark interior and be well lit by the sun, moon or outdoor lighting. To create a dark pool, you can use a black, flexible rubber pond liner, a dark plaster interior finish or tiles that are gray, black or very dark blue.

For added interest, a beautiful tree or a striking piece of art can placed at the far end of a pool, providing it directly catches the rays of the sun or is uplit at night. You can also set a vertical stone column or a tall pot within a reflecting pool and allow water to trickle down from its top intermittently. This action will disturb the water just enough to prevent any mosquitoes from taking up residence.

Don't have room for a reflecting pool? You can use a simple jug or large jar to hold clear water and float seasonal flowers atop it, as art collector Silas Mountsier does in his wonderful garden in Nutley, New Jersey, to great effect! The play of light creates a dramatic reflection despite the small size of the container.

Sunflowers float in a small reflecting jug at the Silas Mountsier garden.

The Japanese Tsukubai

Water has been used for centuries by many traditions to bless or "cleanse" a person or place. In Japan, the act of purifying with water is called *misogi* and traces its origin to a tale about a primordial god who cleansed himself of earthly "tarnishing" with water. The belief that water rids us of the impurities of the world is the basis for the stone water basins common in traditional Japanese tea gardens. Known as a *tsukubai* or "stooping basin," the simple granite bowl is placed near a teahouse to help people literally and spiritually remove the "dust of the world." The water basin is deliberately set low on the ground so guests must crouch down to wash their hands it, promoting the proper humble attitude desired for the tea ceremony. Thus, it is customary to plant very low-growing plants near a *tsukubai*, because it is here where they can be admired up close.

I created this recirculating "tsukubai" fountain to add interest in a quiet, shady garden.

Although we in the West do not use a *tsukubai* for washing hands, the Japanese stone basin can be used as a fountain to create a sweet scene in a garden. Water gently streams over the stone basin into a decorative stone reservoir beneath. It recirculates by way of an underground pump that feeds water through a bamboo conduit pipe back into the bowl.

Isamu Noguchi's *Water Stone*

Isamu Noguchi (1904-1988), the renowned Japanese-American sculptor, produced a modern

version of a *tsukubai,* called *Water Stone,* for the Japan Galleries of the Metropolitan Museum in 1986. He created it from the local basalt stone found near his studio on Shikoku Island, Japan. Like traditional stone basins found in Japanese

This lovely *tsukubai* is at the Portland Japanese Garden in Portland, Oregon, a 5.5 acre public garden, proclaimed to be the most authentic Japanese garden outside of Japan.

gardens, *Water Stone* sits upon a bed of rocks and instills a meditative mood through gently flowing water. Noguchi crafted a modern irregular shape composed of alternating angular polished planes cut into the stone. The water flows up into the basin at the top of the stone (via a pump), appears to come to a standstill, then cascades over the edge, clinging to the angular sides as it falls. *Water Stone* is mesmerizing to look at and conveys the Taoist verse from the *Tao Te Ching, chapter 36:* "The gentle and soft overcomes the hard and aggressive." You can see Noguchi's sculpture at the Metropolitan Museum in New York City.

*   *   *

One thing you will have noticed in this chapter is how much the enjoyment of water in a garden depends on its relationship with stone – the interplay of the transparent and transient with the solid permanence of the hard stone. The textural counterpoint of smoothness and the rough are an age-old pairing, and nowhere is it better displayed than in a garden designed for inspiration and reflection. The next chapter will consider the beauty and meaning of stone in a garden. ❧

FIVE

A Rock's Resonance

There is life in a stone. Any stone that sits in a field or
lies on a beach takes on the memory of that place.
– Andy Goldsworthy

enjoy sitting on a large boulder, feeling its unmovable presence and pondering its timelessness. Dimpled by time, these "ancient ones" tell the story of the land in every fissure and crevice. Perhaps this is what induced naturalist Loren Eiseley to write his eloquent remembrance in *The Firmament of Time:* "....The huge stones were beasts, I used to think, of a kind that man ordinarily lived too fast to understand. They seemed inanimate because the tempo of the life in them was slow. They lived ages in one place and moved only when man was not looking."

Rocks silently resound with the energy of a place and "ground" us with their unwavering earthiness. When we incorporate a large rock into a garden, we infuse the area with stability and power. This power was honored by Native Americans, who addressed large boulders as "Grandfather" or "Aged One." In the traditions of many ancient cultures, stones have been "memory keepers." The ancient Greeks had their sacred *omphalos*, the Mexican Zapotecs revered their obsidian talking stone, and Tibetans still worship *mani* stones.

To the 21st-century mind, revering rocks may seem a little strange, but after working with them as a landscape designer for 40 years, I have developed a special fondness for rocks and understand what these cultures admire. I know I'm not alone. A Native American, Lame Deer, made this perceptive observation:

"You are always picking up odd-shaped stones, pebbles and fossils, saying that you do this because it pleases you, but I know better. Deep inside you there must be an awareness of the rock power, of the spirits in them, otherwise you would not pick them up and fondle them as you do." (From his book, *Lame Deer: Seeker of Visions.)*

A Rock Garden of Peace

The International Garden of Peace is on a sunny hilltop overlooking the glorious Ojai Valley in California, a place so beautiful that it was used as the location for Shangri-la in the movie classic *Lost Horizon*. The Peace Garden is a central feature of Meditation Mount, a hilltop facility open to the public that

The International Garden of Peace Garden in Ojai, California.

82

The plants have grown back once again in the Peace Garden and are now fairly lush.

offers the garden as a place "where people will find inspiration to lead more purposeful and compassionate lives." There is no higher purpose for a garden than that!

The beauty of this drought-tolerant landscape lies partly in the stillness of the large native rocks that dominate the setting. As you enter through a handcrafted arbor and walk down a sinuous path flanked by pinkish-hued boulders, sculptural plants and ornamental grasses, you feel the energy of the faraway vista and the grounding of the solitary stones. The boulders are a perfect complement to the open sky and sit immovable, reflecting sun and moon throughout the seasons. In late 1999, the garden was damaged by a brush fire, but the rocks, ever present, stood watch while the hardy plants grew back stronger than ever. It is fitting then that the management of Meditation Mount decided to inscribe certain boulders in the garden with its six principles of a fulfilled life: "Right Human Relations," "Goodwill," "Group Endeavor," "Unanimity," "Spiritual Approach" and "Essential Divinity." The rocks now bear a message for the ages.

Playing with "Word Stones"

If you like the idea of leaving a message in stone in your garden you can easily buy rounded stones with single words etched into them. You can buy several of these and string phrases or ideas of your own that can be funny, thoughtful or exotic. Following is a list of some of the most popular word inscriptions:

Aloha, Always, Art, Balance, Believe, Bliss, Create, Earth, Easy, Eden, Enjoy, Faith, Forever, Inspire, Imagine, Joy, Kindness, Listen, Love, Peace, Pleasure, Prosper, Relax, Respect, Serenity, Shine, Smile, Spirit, Soar, Think, Thrive, Trust, Unity, Vision, Welcome, Wish, Wonder, Yes

Scatter fifteen or more "word stones" in a group somewhere in your yard. Place them on a bench or wall and encourage visitors to create a stone word phrase. The next person to come along can change the phrase as they wish. This quiet exercise brings out the philosopher – or the comedian – in everyone.

Rock Outcrops and Rock Crevice Gardens

I have learned to love rock outcrops – which is a good thing, since I live in the Northeast United States, home of many rock outcrops. I find that often the best way to deal with rocky sites is to unearth the rock, wash it off and let it "shine" for all the world to admire. Sometimes when we do this we find some real treasures. The rock in the photo to the right is evidence of a glacier's actions and appears almost like flowing water! It is so evocative that, once my clients saw this gem, they chose to keep it exposed.

But what can you do with a rocky site when you want some green or color as well? In the rock garden at the New York Botanical Garden, they

This rock almost appears like flowing water due to the pressure of an ancient glacier against its surface.

Rather than hide this gorgeous rock outcrop I cleared around it and let it proudly show off its shape and mossy surface.

have managed to grow a mix of Japanese Kurume azaleas atop a prominent rock (see photo opposite page). The various cotton candy colors are joyful in the spring when they bloom and this shows what an adaptable plant an azalea can be! To create this effect you should prune them after

Japanese Kurume azaleas drape over a rock outcrop at the wonderful rock garden in the New York Botanical Garden.

flowering and also "tip prune" them again in the summer. Constant pinching will help a Kurume azalea hug a rock like this.

In one landscape that I still work on there is a steep slope punctuated with rocky protrusions everywhere. Next to the house there is a lovely spot, sheltered by tall oaks; I placed a small sitting deck here, nestling directly into the rocky hillside. The carpenter scribed each decking board so that it fits against the protruding 5-foot-high outcrop, making the deck seem like an outgrowth of the hillside. The combination of being protected by the tall rock while enjoying a view makes one feel secure and enthralled at the same time. It is the most comfortable and calming place to sit in the property. And it is also a lovely garden site because I decided to create a "crevice garden" here.

The rock outcrop has many long fissures in it at eye level and so provides a good venue for a crevice garden. The grooves are narrow and shallow and act as natural planting pockets. I fill each crevice with a little bit of lightweight soil mix and plant low growing annuals and perennials (see my plant list below). I use only plants growing in small pots (3" diameter or smaller) in order to be able to fit them in the crevices. I remove the small plants from the containers and gently spread out their roots before inserting them in the soil pocket. You can also use seed here. For an added display, every year I plant annual flowers in prominent pockets in front. The long blooming annuals cloak the rock outcrop in fabulous color all summer.

This is a crevice garden I planted. Every year a few items need to be replaced but what a show it offers all summer!

Some Plants For A Rock Crevice Garden

Botanical Name	Common Name	Description
Aubrieta deltoides	Rockcress	6" high, white
Brachycome iberidifolia	Swan River Daisy	Blue
Gypsophila repens	Creeping Baby's Breath	6" high, white
Sedum spurium 'Dragon's Blood'	Dragon's Blood Stonecrop	6" high, pink
Sedum spurium 'Tricolor'	Tricolor Sedum	Red, green and pink
Sedum kamtschaticum 'Weihenstephaner Gold'	Weihenstephaner Gold Sedum	Golden leaves
Thymophylla tenuiloba	Dahlberg Daisy	12" high, bright yellow
Viola 'tricolor'	Johnny-jump-up	5" high, purple, blue

Little Sparta: The Timeless Appeal of Inscribed Stone

The modern Scottish artist Ian Hamilton Finlay (1925–2006) elevated inscribing words in stone to a high art. Words and phrases etched in stone can be found in his garden, "Little Sparta," located in a pastoral moorland near Edinburgh. Finlay, a fan of classical philosophy, etched sayings that would cause a visitor to pause and think. For example, as you walk along a path, you read two lines inscribed into an upright stone:

MAN
A PASSERBY

These three words affirm or perhaps question your presence there.

Ian Hamilton Finlay's inscribed stone features etched sayings that cause a visitor to pause and think.

Over the course of 25 years, Finlay used his writer's sensibility to transform an old farm into a world of plants, stone, and words, filled with layers of meaning – a poet's garden. (Now open to the public on certain days; see their website.) One stone, set along a rough walk up to the garden, tells you, "The way up and the way down is one and the same." This observation sets the stage for his delightful stonework poems and architectural fragments located amidst Little Sparta's sunken gardens and grassy ponds.

A Latin phrase affixed to a tree in Little Sparta.

Finlay's "concrete poetry," as he called it, was his way to visually convey classical thoughts of harmony. He chose a Roman style typeface for his inscriptions which add an extra dimension to the message These enduring words remind us that a human touch lies behind a garden and uplifts it into an arena of ideas as much as a place of renewal. Indeed, walking around a corner and coming upon a stone inscribed with a word or saying can spark a thought, initiate a chat, or just bring a smile.

Stone Poems in Asian Gardens

A Chinese stone inscription, suitable for making a rubbing from it. Located in Innisfree, Millbrook, NY.

Asian gardens have long featured artful inscriptions in stones. In Japan, short poems called *haiku* are engraved in large rocks and placed in a central spot. These brief poems are spare in style and are often spoken in a single breath, a fleeting moment in time. The Portland Japanese Garden in Oregon features a stone *haiku* by the Japanese poet Shuoshi Mizuhara (1892–1981), written during a visit there in 1966. It is inscribed in a dark gray, smooth stone using the Japanese pictorial characters known as kanji. The spacing of the characters is as important as the tranquil thoughts they convey. Translated, the *haiku* reads:

> Here, miles from Japan
> I stand as if warmed by the
> spring sunshine of home.

In China, stone inscriptions of an image or poem often are set vertically within a wall or on a solitary standing stone. Visitors can transfer the image onto rice paper through stone rubbings. They lay a sheet of paper over the engraved image and color it forcefully with dark ink or crayon to create an exact copy of the picture. These rubbings are considered works of art and are displayed in a home as a reminder of the garden.

Inscribing a Stone for Your Garden

The ancient Norse, Celts, South Americans, Egyptians, and Chinese, among others, all left indelible markings etched in stone. You can also create a lasting garden artifact by carving your own words, image, or symbols in stone using a chisel and mallet. It is not difficult to inscribe an image into a soft stone such as limestone or sandstone. With a waxy crayon, draw the image you want to create and, wearing the appropriate safety gear, carefully incise your lines into the stone with a chisel and a mallet. You can install the inscribed slab upright within a wall or prop it up with a metal frame anchored into the ground. Once complete, this stone will be available to anyone who wants to make a rubbing.

Stacked Stones: A Fun Touch

Stacked stones tell others you were there.

Stacking stones, with the smallest one on top, is an age-old global tradition that taps into our universal need to leave a mark, however small, for eternity. Loren Eiseley noted our "fondness for the building of stone alignments, dolmens, and pyramids" in his book *All the Strange Hours*.

He called it "an unconscious 'ancient heritage.'" This inheritance certainly has a practical side: deliberately piled stones, called "cairns" in northern Europe, have been used as navigational markers on foggy coasts, as simple memorials and as markers designating trails or summits. In Mongolia, stacked stone piles, called *ovoos*, are used in religious ceremonies. And in Sedona, Arizona, such stones mark "energy vortices" in the Earth.

In Tibet, cone-shaped *mani* mounds composed of carefully piled stones can be found in villages and along mountain paths. Upon encountering a large *mani*, a Tibetan walks around it in a clockwise, or "sunwise," direction as a prayer for health and protection, and then places a stone on it as an offering. Thus, the stone mound grows taller with every visitor.

You can stack stones anywhere you choose.

Stacked stones add an enchanting touch to any landscape. The sight of a few rocks balanced precariously atop each other can be a delight next to a patio, in a plant bed or at the front door. You can make a tower of smooth stones using water-rounded stones you find along the seashore or from a local pond or river. You can also purchase tumbled stones – sometimes known as Zen stones – from stone suppliers.

To begin, choose a place for your tower where it will not be knocked over. Select an odd number like three, five or seven rocks (odd numbers are pleasing to the eye) and stack them with the largest at the bottom. As you stack, you must find the balance point of each rock. The allure of a stone tower is in the angle and appearance of each stone.

Once you stack a small rock tower it may not stop there. You may become a full-blown enthusiast and begin to create taller and larger stone piles! If friends question why you are stacking stones, just refer them to these words by Antoine de Saint-Exupery: "A rock pile ceases to be a rock pile the moment a single man contemplates it, bearing within him the image of a cathedral."

A more artful use of unworked stones is to make a "stone man" similar to the traditional *inukshuk* created by the Inuit of the Arctic regions. Here, native stones are stacked to represent the image of a man and have become emblematic of a hardy people. Stone men are common across the Arctic and are a welcome sight to one traveling across a featureless landscape as they mark trails, indicate migration routes and warn of impending danger. They also act as a sign of greeting. You can create your own stone man atop a wall or in the middle of a field. It is an enticing way to say hello.

A "stone man" greets you on the shore in Maine.

A Garden of Standing Stones

Standing stones are the sentinels of a garden. Like silent, protective beings, majestic vertical stones speak to us of time, eternity and Earth. Such stones, tall and fissured, can be set as solitary boulders, in a circle or as a procession of stone images along a garden walk. Any vertically grooved or narrow rock that exhibits a unique character can be used as a standing stone in your garden. It can be the "star" of a scene, placed among very low growing grasses or plants. Japanese gardens often have a standing rock that is deliberately set apart in isolation, in order to highlight its inherent beauty. This rock is meant to be admired, alone, for its unique character. Japan's venerable *Record of Garden Making,* or *Sakuteiki,* says these solitary and separated stones, "are best set on a rocky shore, at the foot of a hill, or at the tip of an island." In the

The majesty of standing stones at Innisfree in Millbrook, NY.

case of today's gardens, the rocky shore can be a contained gravel bed and the foot of a hill can be the base of a small rise in the land.

Beatrix Farrand, a landscape designer in the early 20th century, followed this tradition by setting a massive 8-foot-tall stone sculpture at the end of a long walk called The Spirit Path. It is in the garden of Abby and John D. Rockefeller, Jr., in Seal Harbor, Maine. The figure's dramatic presence acts like a standing stone and is a magical beacon, drawing all visitors inexorably to it.

This Eastern influenced landscape at their bluff-top estate, "The Eyrie," is enclosed by a rose-colored serpentine wall and also features a collection of granite "procession" figures, or Guardians, flanking the Spirit Path. Native shrubs and ground covers grow at their base and soften the stone's solidness. The walk is quite striking. It shows how artfully and appropriately rough stone features can be incorporated into a natural setting. The garden, now called The Abby Aldrich Rockefeller Garden, is open to the public in the summer months, by reservation only.

Similarly, there are several coarsely grained, large, upright stones set in a grouping in Kew Gardens in England that form an unforgettable outdoor setting. And in Innisfree in Millbrook, New York, you can find moss-covered standing stones throughout the grounds, such as those shown in photos on the preceding page.

Chinese Taihu Stones

Traditional Chinese gardens have their highly prized version of standing stones in the form of *Taihu* stones. These strangely shaped, upright limestone rocks are riddled with holes created by the eroding action of water and time. They stand like otherworldly artifacts in Chinese walled-in gardens and symbolize the timelessness of mountains. Their hard

A striking Taihu stone can be seen at the U.S. National Arboretum, Washington, DC.

nature and strong verticality are a "yang" counterpoint to soft bamboo and organically shaped ponds and lakes which are considered "yin." The Chinese dualistic yin/yang view of the world is on display in their gardens simply by using stones, plants and water.

Magnetic Attraction in a Zen Garden

The vertical standing stones of Japanese Zen Buddhist gardens are the most important stones in these spare gardens of stone and sand. The *Ishi Shumisen,* or the "immovable mountain at the center of the universe" connotes an island or mountain, and its power lies in its shape, composition and location relative to others. Seen as a Buddha or male stone, it is the first stone set in place when making the garden and it is typically tall with steep sides and vertical angular lines. It is commonly composed of dark-gray granite or other igneous rock that has formed beneath the surface of the earth's crust.

It is significant that the Buddha stone is formed of igneous rock because such rocks are strongly paramagnetic. This means they have a well-defined positive magnetic force field and affect the space and magnetic flow around them. In a Zen garden the standing stone is always accompanied by a large flat stone called the "Worshiping Stone,"

set in the ground next to it. This is considered a female stone, is lighter colored and often

A granite standing stone "harmonizes" life forces in a garden I designed. The variegated sedge around it adds softness to the scene.

A low, earth-hugging rock is a good counterpoint to the greenery in a garden.

contains white quartz, a weakly diamagnetic stone. Diamagnetism is the negative opposite to paramagnetism and does not have an aligned force field. The dialogue between the standing "male" stone and the horizontal "female" stone may therefore be more than an aesthetic consideration – it may be an energetic counterbalance of yang positive polarity to yin negative polarity. Japanese geomancy is certainly at work in their Zen gardens.

Rocks in these gardens, therefore, reflect a deep understanding of the geomagnetic properties of stone and its impact on a place. With their carefully thought-out rock groupings and varying stone composition, the paramagnetic nature of the standing stones enables these gardens to resonate to the geomagnetic pull of the sun, moon,

and earth. As Marc Keane writes in his book *Sakuteiki: Visions of the Japanese Garden: A Modern Translation of Japan's Gardening Classic*, a Japanese garden "was not just a point of aesthetics, it was an attempt to harmonize one's household with the life forces of the surrounding environment through the design of the garden." This eye-opening concept may explain why standing stones are deemed to be beneficial by so many cultures.

But then again, perhaps it's simply the idea that rocks speak to us of permanence. The Japanese-American artist Isamu Noguchi was a master of stone sculpture; his carved rocks are often sited in beautiful outdoor settings, like Storm King Art Center in Mountainville, N.Y., and the Noguchi Museum in Long Island City, NY.

I visited the Noguchi Museum on a snowy afternoon and saw how – even in winter – stone can evoke a feeling of timelessness and endurance.

This stone sculpture by Japanese-American artist Isamu Noguchi, is quietly alluring even when covered with snow.

Sunwheels, Medicine Wheels and Stone Circles

"Sunwheel" is the term used to describe circles of standing stones such Stonehenge in England and other regions of the world. A sunwheel originally acted as a calendar of sorts by framing a point on the horizon where the sun rose or set at a significant time of year. An iconic circle of huge standing stones served as a sturdy reminder of nature's eternal cycles.

Modern sunwheels in the landscape can be large and elaborate or small and personal. On the shores of Lake Champlain in Burlington, Vermont, you can find the impressive Earth Clock, a 43-foot-diameter circle of standing stones pinpointing sunsets from winter solstice to summer solstice. On the campus of the University of Massachusetts, Dr. Judith Young created an astronomically correct sunwheel using tall, upright stones.

Sunwheels do not have to be large installations. Certain Native American tribes build a traditional form of stone circle called a "medicine wheel." It consists of small stones arranged in a circle with four larger stones set on the perimeter to locate the cardinal directions. A cross of stones within the circle connects the four directional points to denote the center of the wheel. The tallest stone is placed at the center and represents the pivot point of the universe, so to speak.

Each compass point on the wheel has a different connotation:

- The stone in the east represents birth, air, beginnings, spirit, clarity.
- The stone in the south represents youth, fire, journeys, emotions, faith.
- The stone in the west represents maturity, water, dreams, discipline, testing.
- The stone in the north represents the culmination of a cycle, wisdom, listening, elders, Earth.

You can make a form of medicine wheel of any size to add mysterious beauty and grace to your garden. After you clear and level the ground, make your stone circle and locate the four cardinal directions. You can also place 12 large stones in an outer circle to represent the months of the year. Many wonderful variations are possible.

Resonance within a Quartz Stone Circle

Interestingly, if you make a stone circle with stones that contain a predominance of quartz, you may instill a vibrational humming within people who enter this space! Quartz, the most common crystal on the face of the planet, is found in all types of rocks – igneous, sedimentary, and metamorphic. It is "piezoelectric," which means that quartz oscillates, or vibrates, when acted upon by an outside force. For example, quartz crystals are used in watches because they produce a reliable and precise vibration when acted upon by the watch battery.

Veins of white quartz crystal are easy to see in a rock.

Our bones are also piezoelectric and respond to outside stimuli. The cells in our bones and the quartz molecular structure in rocks vibrate in close range to each other. In other words, they are "resonant." So when one vibrates at its natural frequency, it can compel the other into the same vibrational motion. This remarkable property explains why sensitive people can literally feel their bodies – or, more specifically, their bones – vibrating when they stand on a rock outcrop containing large amounts of quartz-crystal. I have a friend who often goes up to a rocky, quartz-encrusted high point just to feel that humming sensation.

Close-up of quartz crystal.

Romancing the Stones:
Guidelines for Rock Placement in a Garden

In every garden I create, I draw detailed landscape plans that address dimensions, grading, drainage, and more. But they are of no help when creating a rock garden or rock strewn hillside. Placing large rocks must be done "in the field" and is a matter of following a stone's wordless instructions more than anything else. It is a true collaboration between gardener and stone, no matter the size of the rock or the style of the garden.

My three design pointers for placing a rock in a garden are (1) bury a stone deep enough so that it does not look like it is sitting atop the ground; (2) place rocks singly or in groups of three, five or seven, and so on; and (3) align the grain or lines of the stone with the overall surroundings. In the garden shown here, I retrieved a boulder from the site, set it in place at an angle to resemble a native rock outcrop and buried half of it. The variegated Maiden grass (*Miscanthus sinensis* 'Variegatus') and rounded river stones were added to provide a textural contrast.

I generally like to use stones that contain some granite. Coarse granite is a hard igneous stone formed during the fiery beginnings of our planet. It provides a stable, restful and grounding presence, known as the "gift of granite." If the granite stone contains a vein of white quartz crystal, so much the better!

I buried this stone so that it looked like a natural outcrop.

Stone Walls: Living Boundaries

A mosaic of stones in a rough stone wall.

A stone wall adds to the personality of a garden. In China, the word for "wall" is the same as the word for "city"; a wall, then, defines what it contains and becomes synonymous with it. This is true also in gardens, where a wall made of stone stands as a living boundary and – more than any other element – forms the personality of the space.

Stone walls, seamed in wavy or straight lines, coalesce into a mosaic that can become colored in time with patches of lichen and moss.

Hydrangeas set off this wall in a client's property so nicely. Hard and soft together always grab the eye.

The rocks may be rough, fractured, or smooth, large or small, depending on what the stone-wall-maker intends. Some walls composed of many small stones look intricate and detailed. This type of wall contrasts beautifully with large-leaved plants like hosta, colocasia or rhododendrons. A more massive wall, constructed from large rocks, can be imposing but you can temper this by planting climbing hydrangea (*Hydrangea anomala* spp. *petiolaris*) on it or draping willowleaf cotoneaster (*Cotoneaster salicifolius* 'Willowleaf") over it. A stately wall, composed of smooth stones carefully fitted together, is an elegant addition to a landscape and can stand alone as a design feature in its own right.

The details of a stone wall can bring "flavor" and interest to a scene. For example, capping a wall with smooth stones that overhang the wall on both sides by a few inches injects formality to a garden. The capstones you choose may be a different kind of stone from the wall. Limestone, bluestone or concrete atop a stone wall make it suitable to sit on. Or, if you have a retaining wall that holds back a hill, you can "batter" it, which means that it is not upright but slopes back at an angle. A battered stone wall is a compelling landscape

A stately stone wall with climbing hydrangea.

Different stone walls in various landscapes I designed – each has its own personality to match the particular setting.

feature and a strong counterforce to a steep hillside. The various stone walls shown here and on the previous page are in landscapes I have designed and that my firm, Johnsen Landscapes & Pools, has built. Each wall's appearance differs according to its setting.

*   *   *

As you can see, I'm an advocate of bringing rocks into a garden setting. Please don't hesitate to use rocks and boulders as objects of art in your garden. Blending rocks with plants and paving is a unique way to add interest and solidity to plant beds, open lawns and enclosed urban terraces. You can set unusual boulders among low plants, pile rounded pebbles in a mound or place straight-edged bluestone flush with the ground in a linear layout. There are all manner of ways to incorporate stone artfully into a garden. I hope this chapter has whetted your appetite for adding a rock's resonance to your surroundings.

If rocks are the bones of a garden, then color is its spark. And that is what the next chapter will explore: color…in all its vivid or muted glory. 🪴

SIX

Color – Nature's Catalyst

*The whole world, as we experience it visually, comes to us through
the mystic realm of color. Our entire being is nourished by it.*

– Hans Hoffman

Color rules a garden in more ways than one. A landscape awash in color catches our eye, sends silent cues to birds, insects and animals, and affects us all with its intensity and contrast. For example, as we're admiring the brilliant red center of a hibiscus flower, the pollinating insects are being told in vivid terms where to zero in for the nectar. The entire natural world, including us, reacts to the language of color.

Red flowers in my backyard excite the eye.

I deliberately used many colors in this garden.

We humans follow color's dictates more than we realize. This became evident to marketing researcher and pioneer, Louis Cheskin, in 1948 when he changed the package color of Jelke's "Good Luck" margarine from white to yellow. The new color improved the sales of Jelke's margarine so dramatically that, since then, almost every brand of margarine and butter has been wrapped in yellow!

This simple color change worked because we universally respond to color, both physically and emotionally. Red instills excitement. Blue evokes calm. Green is restful. These color messages create a mood with their hues and brightness. But you have to know how to use them wisely because, as Louis Cheskin noted, "The right colors are silent music; the wrong colors irritate and disturb."

Color Therapy in the Garden

Distinct colors are varying frequencies of light; they affect us through "vibrational" rates of light energy. Violet is the shortest wavelength of visible light while red is the longest. All the other colors of the visible rainbow of light lie between

Dale Chihuly's colored glass floating sculptures mesmerize in a garden pond.

Vibrant colors like these affect our emotions and more.

these two wave-lengths. Together, they comprise the sunlight that energizes life on this planet.

The vibration of color triggers our brains to release specific biochemicals that, in turn, affect our health and feelings. Once you know how each color affects people's reactions, you can use this knowledge to create a specific mood in any garden.

The ancient Egyptians and Greeks knew about the therapeutic use of color and built healing temples of light and color. It is said that the Egyptians had color-healing rooms built into their temples. Gems such as rubies and sapphires were placed into the walls so that as the sunlight shone through them, the resulting color was used to heal specific ailments.

The European Gothic cathedral builders' use of stained glass, in my opinion, continued this tradition. And we find in traditional Indian Ayurvedic medicine the belief that each energy center of the body, or chakra, is governed by a specific color frequency in the visible light spectrum. The colors red, orange, yellow, green, blue, indigo and violet each correspond to a primary energy center of the body.

Following is a brief synopsis – traditional, scientific and anecdotal – of the effects these major colors have on us, with examples of plants of that color.

Red

Red is the color of excitement, power and luck. Studies show that red stimulates our bodies to pump out adrenaline, which increases blood pressure and pulse rate. Red's arousal effect helps to project an air of confidence; this is why men wear red "power ties" and women wear red suits. As fabric designer and colorist Jack Lenor Larsen noted, "Of all the hues, reds have the most potency."

The American painter Norman Rockwell knew about the power of red and always inserted a small spot of red in each of his pictures to create movement and draw the eye around. A splash of red is all that is needed to catch our attention. You can use this to spice up a plant bed. Draw the eye by planting red foliage or red flowers in various spots.

I placed a bright red accent (Red Cockscomb) in a flower bed.

A red bridge in the Steinhardt Garden, Bedford, NY.

Hindus believe that visualizing red affects the chakra at the base of the spine and strengthens our will. In China, red means good luck and feng shui advisors recommend using red in the southern area of any space. Red doors are considered beneficial in Chinese and other traditions, signifying welcome or a holy place; a red bridge is a traditional feature in Chinese gardens.

Red plants include red rose-mallow (*Hibiscus moscheutos*), red New Guinea impatiens, red-leaved coral bells (Heuchera), red-leaved coleus, scarlet salvia (*Salvia splendens*), and of course, the common red geranium – among many others!

Orange

People generally either love or hate orange; there seems to be little in-between response to this intense, vibrant color. It is the hottest, most flamboyant color in the spectrum and radiates fun. Orange is a true stimulant, increasing oxygen to the brain, exciting the emotions, and even increasing our appetite.

Orange daylilies add a vibrant summer touch.

Orange has been found to encourage people to talk and socialize. Feng shui advises using orange in the southern and southwestern areas of a space to promote lively conversations. Following this advice, it might be a good idea to plant orange flowers or shrubs around an outdoor sitting area.

The softer shades of orange, such as peach, tangerine and apricot, are very attractive in a garden and blend beautifully with blue and gray foliage. These mellow tones are appealing in the warm light of sunset, when they seem to positively glow. This is especially true at the end of summer as the days ripen into the coolness of fall.

In Hindu tradition, orange is the color associated with the sacral chakra, right below the belly button. Focusing on orange, they believe, can increase positive emotions like joy, enthusiasm and creativity.

Orange butterfly weed is the larval host for Monarch butterflies.

Many perennial plants have orange blooms. These include garden phlox 'Orange Perfection' *(Phlox paniculata* 'Orange Perfection'), California poppy 'Aurantiaca' *(Escholzia californica* 'Aurantiaca') and butterfly weed *(Asclepias tuberosa).*

Orange-leaved plants include Scotch heather 'Copper Splendor' *(Calluna vulgaris* 'Copper Splendor'), Coppertina™ ninebark *(Physocarpus opulifolious* 'Mindia') and 'Orange Dream' Japanese maple *(Acer palmatum* 'Orange Dream').

The intoxicating color of a light orange rose.

Yellow

The yellow blossoms of the 'Goldsturm' black-eyed Susan sing in a summer border.

Yellow is the happy color. When we are surrounded by this cheerful, optimistic color our brain releases the "feel good" chemical serotonin. Laughing also releases serotonin. If you are feeling out of sorts, perhaps a yellow garden and a funny thought can lift your spirits. As it says in Proverbs 17:22, "A merry heart doeth good like a medicine." Yellow is good medicine.

The color yellow also enhances our mental processes and clarity of mind. This is thought to be the reason why yellow was chosen as the original color of the common legal pad of paper. It may also be why most of the graphite pencils in the United States are painted yellow.

Yellow governs the solar plexus chakra, center of vitality. It inspires creativity; in feng shui it is thought to enrich the emotions. It is associated with the center of a space, brightening any area and curing it of sluggish energy.

So if you want a cheery and vibrant garden, plant lots of yellow flowers and foliage! There is a multitude to choose from. These include Goldfink coreopsis (*Coreopsis grandiflora* 'Goldfink'), dwarf 'Teddy Bear' sunflower (*Helianthus annuus* 'Teddy Bear'), dwarf black-eyed Susan (*Rudbeckia fulgida* var. *sullivantii* 'Goldsturm'), petunia 'Supertunia® Citrus', and golden creeping Jenny (*Lysimachia nummularia* 'Aurea').

The dazzling yellow Jacaranda tree.

Green

Green balances and alleviates anxiety.

Green, the pervasive color of Nature, is known as the "master color" of peace and renewal. It is the most restful color to our eye and is associated with love and beauty. The Roman goddess of love, Venus, is signified by green, as is the heart chakra. Hindus say that imagining green will allow more emotional balance and empathy to enter your life. Russell Page, the great English landscape designer, used green to describe gardeners as compassionate souls, saying in his book, The Education of a Gardener, "Green fingers are the extension of a verdant heart."

Green balances and alleviates anxiety. Thus, being in a green space is good for relaxation. In feng shui, green represents revitalization and new beginnings. It is recommended for use in the eastern and southeastern areas of a space.

Interestingly, our eyes can discern more shades of green than any other color.

Green abounds in a garden. Notable green-leaved plants include 'Ruffles' elephant ear (*Colocasia esculenta* 'Ruffles'), green sedum (*Sedum kamtschaticum*) and Christmas fern (*Polystichum acrostichoides*). Photo at left is 'Blue and Gold' *Tradescantia*.

We can see more shades of green than any other color.

Blue

Annual blue Salvia turns deeper blue in cool fall weather.

Blue is everyone's "favorite color." It is, hands down, the most popular color worldwide, having equal appeal to both men and women. No one knows why blue is so popular, but perhaps it is because we see

Blue hydrangeas are everyone's favorite.

blue overhead in the sky daily. Restful and calm, it is the color of tranquility. Scientists have found that looking at blue aids both our concentration and intuition. Blue rooms are known to enhance creative tasks such as brainstorming and problem solving.

Deep blue is often associated with distinction and as a signature of authority. Interestingly, the White House has had an oval-shaped "Blue Room," used for receptions, since 1837. In Hindu belief, blue governs the throat chakra and symbolizes communication. Feng shui advises using deep blue in the northern, eastern and southeastern areas of a space.

Purple and Violet

Purple connotes magic and higher wisdom. Being a blend of red and blue, this popular color has shades that range from an indigo-blue-purple to a violet-red-purple. All shades of purple and violet are associated with originality and uniqueness. Purple is giving blue a run for its money as the second favorite color worldwide.

Since ancient times, purple has symbolized royalty. Roman emperors used it as their color, as do modern European kings and queens. In Hinduism, the color indigo-purple governs the pineal gland or third eye chakra while

'Amethyst Beauty' clematis creates a splash.

violet-purple is associated with the crown chakra at the top of the head. Focusing on any form of purple quiets the mind's chatter. In feng shui, purple is used in healing and meditative spaces. Interestingly, it is said that Leonardo da Vinci believed that the light streaming through purple stained-glass windows could increase the power of meditation tenfold!

Purple flowers and foliage adds substance to a garden. The color purple separates and defines other colors and creates a powerful sense of drama to its surroundings. Notable purple plants for a garden include 'Prince' coral bells *(Huechera 'Prince'),* 'Velvet Cloak' Smokebush *(Cotinus coggygria* 'Velvet Cloak'*),* and purple pansies *(Viola* x *wittrockiana).*

I planted purple 'Angelface' Angelonia behind white wax begonias for a great effect.

A Brief Overview of Color's Impact on Us

	Red	Orange	Yellow	Green	Blue	Purple/Violet
Emotional	Invokes courage and confidence	Promotes socialization and talking	Enhances clarity of thought and brightens mood	Nourishes emotional balance and health	Creates a restful, calming atmosphere	Fosters inner quietude
Physical	Increases blood pressure, heartbeat and pulse rate	Invigorates oxygen to the brain, invigorating and stimulating the appetite	Triggers the brain to release serotonin, the "feel good" chemical	Helps alleviate depression, nervousness and anxiety	Enhances focus, lowers heart rate	Integrates both brain hemispheres for unity of vision
Symbolism	Love, romance, passion	Warmth, energy, enthusiasm, creativity	Cheerfulness, clarity of mind, enlightenment	Peace, harmony, renewal	Dependability, dignity, steadfastness	Originality, distinction, spirituality
Chakra	Root chakra (base of spine): the color of "grounding"	Sacral chakra; the color of fertility, creativity	Solar Plexus chakra: the color of vitality, personal will	Heart chakra: the color of compassion, balance	Throat chakra: the color of communication	Third eye chakra: the color of inner guidance
Feng Shui	Attracts prosperity: use in south areas of a space	For lively conversations: use in south and southwest areas	Wakes up sluggish energy: use in center of a space	For renewal and new beginnings: use in east and southeast areas	Deep blue for serenity: use in north, east areas	For use in healing and meditative spaces
Cultural Notes	The color of luck and prosperity in China	Safety orange: used for traffic cones and other marking devices	The popular color for school buses, pencils and cabs	The color of Venus, Roman goddess of love, beauty; in Japan, the color of eternal life	The color of Mary in Christian religiious iconography	Purple Heart is for courage in battle; seen as a royal color

A chart showing the significance of certain colors.

Using Single-Color Garden Schemes to Inspire and Enthrall

I planted a mass of cool blue Salvia to be calming.

Color is the first thing we notice in an outdoor space. You can create a specific feeling almost immediately with colorful flowers and foliage. Cool colors such as blues, purples, whites and greens form a serene atmosphere. Warm colors – yellows, reds, oranges and warm pinks – liven up a garden and catch our eye.

But how to sort them out and achieve the effects we want? To begin with, let's look at some monochromatic schemes that feature one dominant color. These can be entrancing.

Elegant and sublime? Think about a predominantly white garden with snowy, opalescent flowers and foliage; it will positively glow in the evening.

Mysterious? A blue garden, dotted with deep and light hues of blue flowers against the sky, may be the most mysterious of them all!

Meditative and restful? That would be a green-themed garden.

I should mention that since plants and flowers are tinted with several colors rather than being shades of a single color, it is nearly impossible to create a purely one-color garden. For this reason, a blue garden may be blue and purple and a white garden may be white and light yellow.

Green-hued shrubs add serenity to the garden.

The Crisp Sparkle of a White Garden

A white garden invites you in to savor the subtle atmosphere. It elevates but does not overwhelm. The atmosphere speaks to us of innocence and new possibilities. White, the most versatile color in the landscape, cools us down on a hot summer day and sparkles in the dark evenings of October. Feng shui calls it the color of purity and ancient yogi tradition considers white one of the supreme colors.

White 'Limelight' hydrangea stands out against a dark green backdrop of evergreen 'Emerald' arborvitae.

The idea of a white garden has always had its charm. While most people lean towards colorful borders and exuberant planters, many among us look to white flowers and foliage as a balm to soothe the spirit. Vita Sackville West, the erudite English garden writer, said it best:

"White flowers are anathema to all but the oldest and most sophisticated of gardeners."

This is a sly way to say that only the most refined of gardeners prefer white. And Vita would know; she created the best known white garden in the world at her estate in England, Sissinghurst. Her words, by the way, were the impetus for the name, White Flower Farm, a well-respected mail order plant supplier.

You can introduce white into a garden by planting white flowers, of course, but don't forget

Slender Deutzia *(Deutzia gracilis)* blooms in spring along with the tulips. The graceful, low-growing woody shrub is covered with tiny white flowers.

The white annual flower, 'Serena' angelonia borders this walk that I designed. The 'Wintergreen' boxwood hedge acts as a great backdrop. On certain evenings, the flowers glow in the moonlight.

white-barked trees such white birch and white flowering trees such as dogwoods and crabapples. These trees stand out gloriously against a green backdrop; it is this combination of white and green that we find so refreshing. This holds true for spring flowering white daffodils and white slender deutzia *(Deutzia gracilis)* as they grow amid nascent green foliage to light up the vernal landscape. Along with white deutzia, you can add white Louisiana iris, white Angelonia (a summer blooming annual flower) and the perennial Montauk daisies *(Nipponanthemum*

nipponicum) – to keep the theme of a white garden alive from spring through fall.

I love the tall 'Limelight' Hydrangea *(Hydrangea paniculata* 'Limelight') for its beautiful and reliable white/lime-green flowers, fast growth and easy care. It is hardy to Zone 3, can grow to 10 feet tall and thrives in full sun or partial shade, blooming from mid-summer to frost. Both a wonderful cut flower and landscape plant, it can be pruned into tree form. It will

I created this landscape in phases. This is a part of the "lookout" and the white 'Limelight' hydrangeas dominate the scene. They look great against the natural stone.

flower every year and looks great with compact, fragrant yellow/white Sunny Knockout roses *(Rosa* 'Radsunny') and low grasses. You cannot go wrong with this white flowering gem if you have room for it.

There is also a shorter growing form called 'Little Lime' from Proven Winners that grows 3 to 5 feet tall and wide, about a third to half as big as 'Limelight'. Like its bigger sibling, 'Little Lime's' flowers gradually change from lime-green to pink and make excellent bouquets, fresh or dried. It is especially charming as a container plant; just remember to plant it in a big pot!

Variegated Plants for a White Garden

A white garden can also feature plants that have varie-gated or silvery leaves. Outside my window in the northwest section of my little yard is a variegated dogwood shrub *(Cornus alba* 'Elegantissima').
I prune it back in early spring and then the green and white

Variegated red twig dogwood has green and white leaves and showy red stems in winter, making this an attractive shrub for all seasons! I plant it in front of evergreen trees for an outstanding display.

'Limelight' hydrangeas and 'Sunny Knockout' roses are a great pairing. The slight tinge of yellow in the roses add a bit of interest to this white-blooming combo.

I planted 'Jack Frost' bugloss along with the annual flower, 'Serena' Angelonia in a sunny location. This combination cannot be beat in a white garden – or any garden, for that matter.

leaves grow in to cover the compact bush with a cloak of brightness, which I especially admire in autumn.

My other favorites include 'Jack Frost' Siberian Bugloss *(Brunnera macrophylla* 'Jack Frost')*, named the 2012 Perennial Plant of the Year. This 15-inch-tall, shade-loving perennial has striking heart-shaped silver leaves and sports lovely small blue flowers in spring. It is very hardy, handles a bit more heat and sun than other Brunnera cultivars, and adds a sparkle all season long in the white shade garden.

The variegated Japanese water iris *(Iris ensata* 'Variegata')* offers green and white blades all the way through late October and does well in wet, non-draining situations. It is the perfect perennial plant for any pond setting; I plant them in wet soils at the base of slopes or among rocks where the drainage is poor. Their leaf markings brighten any garden!

The last variegated plant I want to mention is the 'Emerald Gaiety' wintercreeper *(Euonymus fortunei* 'Emerald Gaiety')*. It is with some trepidation I mention this because, although it is a slow-to-medium grower, the wintercreeper family

I like the contrast of the upright blades of the variegated Japanese water iris with the scalloped leaves of the 'Hummelo' variety of wood betony *(Stachys officinalis* 'Hummelo')*.

'Emerald Gaiety' wintercreeper has deep green and white variegated foliage that takes on a rose-red hue in late fall. It will mound when it cannot climb on something. It can soften a stone wall beautifully.

can be considered invasive in some areas. I have never found that with 'Emerald Gaiety,' but I mention it nonetheless. The beauty of this evergreen vining shrub is its bright, cheerful white and green leaves. They stay through the winter and add some white interest to an evergreen planting. It is quite versatile and can be trained as a vine on posts, rocks and along a trellis. They can be grown in sun or shade.

The White Garden: an Evening Delight

White gardens are especially alluring in the evening when they reflect the moonlight. Their compelling brilliance can be seen clearly in a shady garden where the white flowers seem to gleam. For this reason, I often plant a mass of white astilbe 'Deutschland' (Astilbe 'Deutschland') in partial shade conditions to catch the eye from afar.

Astilbes create fern-like mounds of foliage and have plume-like flower panicles on slender, upright stems in late spring. 'Deutschland', a perennial, grows to 18 inches tall and features pure white flowers on 2-foot-tall stems. They look wonderful in the front of a border.

Oakleaf hydrangeas (Hydrangea quercifolia) are stalwart performers in partial shade landscapes. They are native to

I planted a large group of 'Deutschland' astilbe next to 'All Gold' golden Japanese forest grass (Hakonechloa macra 'All Gold') in a shady setting. This combo brightens it up considerably!

In this woodland landscape that I designed I chose to plant a mass of 'Alice' oakleaf hydrangeas along with hay-scented ferns *(Dennstaedtia punctilobula)* for a gracious, woodland feeling. The bench invites you to stop and enjoy the moment.

the southeast U.S. The cultivar 'Alice' is among the tallest of the oakleaf hydrangeas, growing up to 12 feet tall. When the large white blooms appear in mid-summer, they create quite a striking show, especially when planted in a group. At night, the mass of white flowers is stunning. As an added bonus, its oak-like leaves turn a brilliant crimson in fall.

Because white flowers "glow" in dark autumn evenings, I like to place white chrysanthemums in pots by my front door to greet people. I also plant them in plant beds to light up dark corners. The other white flower (with a touch of yellow) that I love in fall evenings is the annual flower, Lantana 'Lucky White'. I plant these out as small plants every spring and enjoy their constant

'Lucky White' Lantana is a constant bloomer all summer long despite heat and drought. Its white and yellow flowers look great against stone and the blue foliage of the dwarf 'Montgomery' blue spruce (*Picea pungens* 'Montgomery').

blooming all the way to frost. 'Lucky White' is a mounding lantana and stands up well to heat and drought. They look great in pots, baskets and in flower beds. In one garden, I placed a round stone finial in a plant bed and planted Lantana 'Lucky White' all around it. It made quite a nice evening accent. Lantana is also a butterfly magnet, a big plus!

The Exotic Allure of a Blue Garden

A blue garden is irresistible to many gardeners. The mix of blue, light-blue and purple flowers creates a sumptuous look and it seems many can't get enough of this color in their gardens. In fact, half of the flowers in seed lists and plant catalogs are some shade of blue, indigo or violet. Feng shui experts say that light blue is the color of harmonious expansion and gentle growth, while darker blue calls up tranquility. No wonder so many of us hanker for a blue garden.

One of the most intriguing blue gardens open to the public is Lotusland, in Santa Barbara, California. This 37-acre botanical gem, filled with an eclectic mix of tropical and subtropical plants, was originally planned as a retreat for Tibetan monks by Madame Ganna Walska, an opera singer and socialite in the mid-20th century. She subsequently divided the property into various theme gardens, each one more fascinating than the one before. The exotic Blue Garden has

Globe Thistle 'Veitch's Blue' (*Echinops ritro* 'Veitch's Blue') is a blue star in a summer garden – great drought tolerant perennial that attracts butterflies and hummingbirds.

paths lined with chunks of blue-green glass (slag from a local bottled-water factory) and an assortment of blue-tinged plants, including a Mexican blue palm, blue Atlas cedar, soft blue fescue, and bold blue succulents.

It's not necessary to have a truly all-blue garden to gain the effects you want. Your own version of a blue garden can use blue's enchanting energy as a "main course" or as a sensory "appetizer." I like to incorporate blue as a border in front of other plants. I often plant large groups of purple-blue succulents like *Sedum* 'Vera Jameson' in a sunny spot or *Lobelia* 'Crystal Palace' in the shade. I

An outstanding weeping blue Atlas cedar in one of my landscapes. The blue needles make quite the show.

also use the blue-needled, evergreen weeping blue Atlas cedar as a striking blue accent. The weeping cedar in one of my clients' landscapes has grown into quite an outstanding specimen!

Blue, being a cool color, tends to recede into the background and needs the help of strong sunlight to hold its own against the flashier warm colors, such as red and yellow. It essentially disappears from view in shady areas but you

The Blue Garden in Lotusland, Santa Barbara, CA.

can counter blue's "shyness" by planting large masses of blue flowering plants. A large swath of blue flowers, such as catmint *(Nepeta nemerosa),* annual blue salvia *(Salvia farinacea),* or miniature 'Blue Chip' butterfly bush *(Buddleia* hybrid 'Blue Chip'),* does not overwhelm the scene as other, brighter colors might.

Blue, unlike other colors, has the distinction of staying "blue" in all its shades. The 20th-century French Painter, Raoul Dufy, explained that blue "will always stay blue; whereas yellow is blackened in its shades, and fades away when lightened; red when darkened becomes brown, and diluted with white is no longer red, but another color – pink."

A background of any sort helps blue plants to stand out. Longwood Gardens, in Kennett Square, Pennsylvania, features a stunning blue border in their "Caryopteris Allee." This straight grassed walk is flanked on both sides by a row of 3-foot-high 'Blue Mist' shrubs *(Caryopteris clando-nensis)* set in front of a dark-evergreen backdrop. When they bloom blue in late summer the view is magical.

You can create the same effect using 'Walker's Low' catmint and planting them in front of a dense evergreen such as arborvitae, yew or euon-ymus – the billowing blue flowers shine against the green (photo at right). Two other blue plants that look great in groups are the vertical 'Heavy

Metal' switch grass *(Panicum virgatum* 'Heavy Metal')* and 'Caesar's Brother' Siberian iris *(Iris sibirica* 'Caesar's Brother').*

More things to plant that boost a garden's intrigue: tall vertical spires of 'Veitch's Blue' globe thistle *(Echinops ritro* 'Veitch's Blue') or tall verbena *(Verbena bonariensis).* For a striking

I planted this border of catmint 'Walker's Low' *(Nepeta racemosa* 'Walker's Low)* for its soft blue flowers in spring.

Allium 'Purple Sensation' is a late spring flowering bulb that adds a regal note with its purple color.

accent, try flowering onion. Nothing beats a row of 3-foot-high 'Sensation' flowering onion (*Allium* 'Purple Sensation') and their spherical, violet flowers.

If you incorporate plants with blue leaves you ensure that blue will be a constant presence in your garden, even when little else is flowering. And blue leaves are outstanding contrasted against blue flowers. For example, the wide leaves of blue hosta remain eye-catching even as they share the stage with the fuzzy flowers of *Ageratum* 'Artist Alto Blue.' The blue-leaved rue (*Ruta graveolens*) is also a nice touch against deep blue 'Caradonna' perennial blue salvia (*Salvia nemerosa* 'Caradonna').

But don't take the idea of "plant only blue flowers or foliage" too seriously, because some-times total blueness can be a little bland. A predominantly blue palette featuring a pinch of grey, a smattering of white and a dollop of creamy vanilla white is a lovely sight indeed. Gertrude Jekyll, the original master of color in the garden, put it best in her book, *Colour Schemes for the Flower Garden,* when she advised, "A blue garden, for beauty's sake, may be hungering for a group of white Lilies, or for something of the palest lemon-yellow." So go ahead and add a few accents of white, grey, or pale yellow in your blue garden!

A great annual flower to mix in with all that blue is *Angelonia angustifolia,* sometimes called "Summer Snapdragon." It grows to about 22 inches tall, has beautiful flowers that bloom into fall, and its variety, 'Wedgewood Blue,' a bicolor blend of blue and white blossoms, adds just the right touch of variation to a blue garden. *Angelonia* 'Angelface White' also stands up to summer heat and remains bright white throughout the season.

'Wedgewood Blue' *Angelonia* blends both white and light purple in its blossoms.

The mystery of a blue gate beckons.

a corner of the property. The particular shade of blue was specifically chosen by my client for its richness and depth. The gate, part of a protective wire-mesh fence hidden amongst a dense shrub border, is set back on a stone cobble landing and flanked by two dark-green boxwoods. I also relocated a large golden threadleaf cypress just beyond the gate to act as a bright yellow-green backdrop. With all these little touches, the "Blue Gate" became an irresistible draw.

Blue cushions, benches and blue tiled tables can add a sweet touch. Silas Mountsier's garden in Nutley, New Jersey, sets blue-cushioned seats against large-textured green foliage to create a dynamic punch, expressing a sort of French provincial *joie de vivre*.

Blue cushions and a tiled table injects a French provincial feeling to a garden.

Thinking beyond plants. Another blue garden favorite is adding a striking blue feature such as a blue chair, blue planter, blue pillow or anything that grabs your fancy. For one client, I installed a blue gate as an entry to a vegetable garden in

'Artist Alto Blue' Ageratum

"Can't Miss" Plants for a Blue/Purple Garden

There is no dearth of blue plants for a serene and inspirational garden! Below are 10 of my favorite blue/purple flowering and foliage plants. I use the term blue loosely here and include blooms that are in the blue/purple family.

1. Artist® 'Alto Blue' floss flower *(Ageratum* 'Artist® Alto Blue'). This ageratum has mounds of fuzzy, lavender-blue flowers on 12-inch to 18-inch-tall plants from late spring through fall. It adds showy, midheight interest. It is grown as an annual flower in colder regions.

2. 'Purple Sensation' flowering onion *(Allium aflatunense* 'Purple Sensation'). This bulb sports round, baseball-sized violet-purple flowers on 30-inch-tall stems. It stateliness adds a sculptural dimension to a spring garden.

3. 'Professor Kippenberg' aster *(Aster dumosus* 'Professor Kippenberg'). This lavender-blue perennial has densely packed clusters of daisy-like flowers covering the plant into late fall. It is a hardy native.

'Professor Kippenberg' Aster

4. 'Boulder Blue' blue fescue *(Festuca glauca* 'Boulder Blue'). Blue fescue is a short, fine-leafed grass known for its intensely blue color. The one-foot-high compact mounds of narrow leaves are incomparable for rock gardens or

'Boulder Blue' Blue Fescue

alongside plants with larger leaves. Best of all, it is drought and heat tolerant.

5. **Tall Verbena** *(Verbena bonariensis).* This outstanding flower is perennial in Zones 7-10 but can be grown as an annual. It makes a statement with tall, willowy stems to 6 feet high that do not need staking. The lilac-purple clusters of flowers bloom from July to frost. They float above all and are excellent for borders. Heat tolerant.

Verbena bonairensis

6. **Hosta 'Hadspen Blue'** (Hosta 'Hadspen Blue'). This perennial adds a vibrant blue to a shady garden; the color intensity does not fade when planted in the shade. It is 15 inches high and 20 inches across, and it is slug resistant.

7. **'Caesar's Brother' Siberian Iris** *(Iris sibirica 'Caesar's Brother').* The spring flowers of Siberian iris live up to their mythical namesake, Iris, the Greek goddess of the rainbow. The deep-blue variety known as 'Caesar's Brother' rises above an elegant clump of grass-like blue-green foliage.

8. **'Walker's Low' Catmint** *(Nepeta x faassenii 'Walker's Low').* This prolific perennial flower billows blue when in bloom in spring and summer. Its foliage is soft blue-gray and looks great with roses.

'Walker's Low' Catmint

9. 'Victoria Blue' annual salvia *(Salvia farinacea* 'Victoria Blue'). This annual flower has deep-blue blossom spikes and blooms nonstop from summer to first frost. For a subtle two-tone effect, plant it with another annual salvia cultivar, 'Rhea' *(Salvia farinacea* 'Rhea'), which has softer blue flowers.

10. 'Crystal Palace' trailing lobelia *(Lobelia erinus* 'Crystal Palace'). The dark-blue flowers of this low-growing, trailing annual flower are dazzling in their vibrancy. They like shade and are best planted where they can be seen up close, among rocks or edging blue lacecap hydrangeas *(Hydrangea macrophylla* 'Blue Wave').

The Restful Call of Green

Green, in all its shades and tones, is the nourishing color of nature. In a garden, we can find lime green twining with moss green, spring green, and more. This verdant, multihued show is especially rich in spring, when refreshing mint greens and emerald greens dot tree limbs, renewing us after a colorless winter.

Green is the color midway on the light spectrum. It calms us with its natural balance of cool and warm undertones. Studies have found that a predominantly green setting soothes our emotions and relaxes our mind. This is why "seafoam" and "fern" green are often painted on hospital-room walls and in bedrooms. Deep forest green, evocative of the silence of the woods, is preferred for dens and studies.

'Dragon's Eye' Pine and 'Blue Chip' juniper make a verdant scene.

A relaxing combination of evergreens and hydrangea.

A "green interlude" garden. A green interlude is a garden-within-a-garden. It creates a restful place to stop and is a good way to separate areas within a large landscape. A planting of evergreens and large textured plants can be the literal pause that refreshes, calming the eye and the atmosphere. Place a bench in this quiet setting to entice visitors to enjoy a "green break" before moving on to more stimulating, active areas.

The best model for a green garden can be found in Japan, where they use green almost to the exclusion of all other colors in their landscapes. Here, green is viewed as representing long life and harmony,

Green Lady's Mantle blends well with azaleas.

and so the varied plant textures of pine, maple, holly, azalea, ferns, and junipers are used often. The greens highlight the passing of each season. In summer, green foliage plays against deep shadows; in winter, evergreen boughs against the contrasting tracery of bare branches generate a meditative atmosphere.

A lovely textural contrast of soft pine needles and Sedum 'Autumn Joy'.

against bold sedums, feathery Threadleaf cypress *(Chamaecyparis)*, graceful iris, and glossy, dark hollies. I planted several of these puffy pillow plants intermittently in front of a long, curving plant border to inject visual rhythm and softness

Ferns. For a shady garden, ferns add luxuriant texture, especially when planted in large groups. I learned how marvelous ferns are in a garden when I designed a patio and deck for John Mickel, a fern expert and author of *Ferns for American Gardens*. After our project was complete, John proceeded to fill his garden with amazing ferns. I learned from him that there is no dearth of ferns to choose from for textural interest. I was struck by the beauty of the ferns he planted along bluestone steps. I also like to intermix 'Fortune's Holly' fern *(Cyrtomium fortunei)* with the evergreen Christmas fern

Ferns grace a stairway.

(Polystichum acrostichoides) and the groundcover, 'Bowles' myrtle *(Vinca minor* 'Bowles') to create a woodland setting.

"Texture echoing." This is my name for a technique often seen in Japanese gardens. Like color repetition in a garden, you can repeat the same leaf shape throughout a scene, drawing the eye around it. Contrasting leaf textures creates a subtle but scintillating effect. For example, the long, soft needles of the 'Blue Shag' dwarf white pine, a low-mounding evergreen, look great

'Fortune's Holly' fern is perfect for a woodland garden.

Color – Making Life a Little Sweeter

Color in a garden may seem to be a trifling subject when compared to other "more important" issues of design. But color, as I have explained, affects us more than we know. If we are aware of color's impact on our psyche we can create serene, harmonious settings where life is a little sweeter. In a 2001 study conducted by Dr. Frances E. Kuo in a Chicago public housing development, women who lived in apartment buildings with trees and greenery outside their buildings reported that they could deal better with major life issues than those living in barren but otherwise identical buildings. Aren't we all like that? The natural color our plants provide, and their vital presence around us, refreshes our ability to cope and gives us the needed "down time" – if only as a view – that we all need. 🌿

Some Last Thoughts

Adopt the pace of nature: her secret is patience.
– Ralph Waldo Emerson

The making of a garden, of any size and type, is an exciting and gratifying venture. Working outdoors with the soil exalts us in some way. This must be why the Latin word for "cultivate," *colere,* means both "to till" and "to cherish." Turning over the soil – cultivating a garden – allows us to cherish Nature and her creative processes. It hones our powers of observation, and while we putter among the plants, pruning, digging, planting, we become more aware of the natural world's inner life. This cultivation of awareness is perhaps the most important aspect of designing an "unhurried" garden. As Frank Lloyd Wright advised, "Study nature. Love nature. Stay close to nature. It will never fail you."

Grass treads lead the eye up, softly. A pleasant spot to study nature's interconnections.

I learned this firsthand as a landscape architecture student at the University of Hawaii. I had an assignment that required me to spend 24 hours in an outdoor spot of my choosing. Within that period of time, I was told to note all that I saw, including the weather, plants, animals, sounds, terrain and anything else that caught my eye. I could not leave the general location for any extended length of time. This exceptional task strengthened my powers of observation immensely, and as I studied my surroundings I witnessed, up close, the interconnectedness of Nature.

Next time you are outside, watch the network of life that inhabits your outdoor environment – the birds, trees, flowers, even lowly earthworms – all filling an essential niche within a harmonious whole. They partake in a miraculous symphony of interlocking parts. By admiring Nature's tapestry, you can develop the singular clarity that Alan Watts, the Buddhist writer, called "vivid awareness." It is from this viewpoint that the best garden design ideas emerge.

Finding Inspiration

If you want to be inspired there is no better way to start than to look at photos of other landscapes.

The lure of a sheltered purple corner. I thought the stone wall we installed was a little too harsh and so I planted hydrangeas to create a lush backdrop for the bench. The bluestone base is curved to match the shape of the seat.

An intriguing stone bridge at the Steinhardt Garden in Bedford, NY. It is open for visits during the Garden Conservancy's Open Days.

Pinterest, Houzz, Facebook, Garden Design, among other websites, are wonderful for this, as are great garden books and magazines. Through remarkable photos you can see how any place – a rocky hill, an urban plot or a suburban yard – can be transformed into a glorious outdoor haven. And dream a little: have you always wanted an outdoor shower? A secret garden? Push monetary considerations aside for a while and let your imagination go.

You should also visit inspiring landscapes such as botanical gardens, zoos, the grounds of various museums, or historic inns or wineries. Even a trip to Disneyworld is a great opportunity because it is a treasure trove of innovative planting design ideas. And don't forget the Garden Conservancy's program called Open Days, which is when local people open their personal gardens to the public for viewing. You can learn so much from these visits.

Nature's Time

In the introduction I mentioned that serene gardens can elicit that exquisite moment I call "stop time." It occurs when the fragrance of a single rose-pink blossom lifts you away or when you step into your backyard and take that first deep breath of crisp morning air. It is that point when time slows down.

Anyone who has lost themselves to a daydream on a sparkling afternoon in a garden knows intuitively that time ebbs and flows. Minutes can stretch as we rake dry, crunchy leaves or snip old

An open garden gate into an exuberant flower garden invites us into a realm where Nature's time rules.

hydrangea blooms. We "lose track of time" as we sip tea and marvel at the nuanced colors of a blossom or enjoy the dance of clouds overhead.

Gardens can also signal the flow of time – daily time, seasonal time and yearly time – by unfurling leaves and bursting buds, by nascent seed pods and frost on glistening evergreens. This is Nature's time, a quiet spiraling of experience that envelops us wholly.

What a contrast this is to its counterpart, our human, mechanical time. Human time is run by the clock and calendar. It divides our days into hours, minutes, seconds, milliseconds. It is, as Alan Lightman writes in his book *Einstein's Dreams,* "as rigid and metallic as a massive pendulum of iron that swings back and forth, back and forth; unyielding, predetermined..." Mechanical time exerts a constant pressure on our lives, superseding all else.

Nature's time, on the other hand, is unrushed. It is as eternal as a granite boulder and as fleeting as a snowflake on a sunny winter day.

It needs no device to measure it. The sun's rays and the moon's waxing and waning are its dutiful keepers. Nature's time affords depth and adds a patina to outdoor elements. Wood grays out and becomes the color of stones over time. Stones become covered with moss and lichen and become the color of the woods. Time burnishes everything with change, wrought by the passing years.

A garden helps us celebrate Nature's time more fully. As Einstein explained, our "place" in the cosmos is not so much a physical site as it is a time frame – our reality a blend of space and time. So I guess the best way to experience Nature's time is, as Ram Dass wrote: "Be here now." Gardens help us do that, in a quiet but glorious way.

It's All in the Way You See

If you are reading this and thinking, "This is all nice, but the only outdoor space I have is a tiny backyard," my heartfelt response to you is, "Any size will do!" Growing up in Brooklyn, New York, my equivalent of a yard was the fire escape outside my window. I filled that outdoor ledge with pots of plants in all sizes and thrilled to it every time I looked out. If that is the extent of your property, then learn all about plants that grow well in containers and have fun finding

Color always steals the show, especially at the height of summer. The purple flowers planted at this high point are the marvelous 'Senorita Rosalita' Cleome.

great planters. As in life, it is the way that you look at your outdoor space that is significant – not the space itself.

And one more thing: there is no such thing as a crazy idea. Years ago, when I was interning at an architecture firm in Japan, I boldly suggested to my boss that we place our latest commission, a modern art museum for the Gutai group of artists, within the side of an existing hill. This unsolicited suggestion from a young woman was a very un-Japanese thing to do, especially decades ago. He thought it over and suggested, very respectfully, that perhaps I was more suited to be a landscape architect. As he sent me away to a landscape architecture office, I thought I had made a terrible blunder by suggesting my "crazy" idea. But it was all for the best, because I found my true vocational calling and I heard that he subsequently used my crazy idea for a well-known Japanese wedding park. You never know where a design idea may come from.

* * *

And so I wish you great happiness in creating a serene and unhurried garden. Creating a garden is one way, among many, to know Nature. You have the opportunity to become the director and overseer of a living world of your own. By your hand, you can determine the lay of the land, the entryways, the plant life, the features and the boundaries. You learn about microclimates and life cycles. You lose track of time observing and tending this place, so full of life. You will always learn something from your time there and you will understand why I say that heaven is a garden. 🍂

Have fun with color! I added blue agapanthus to contrast with the beautiful rock and the vibrant orange daylilies.

Books You Might Find Interesting

Here is an eclectic assortment of books that in some way speak to creating a serene garden in tune with the land, plants and elements. They range from literary to inspirational and include books that are informative or just simply "eye candy." (Shown in alphabetical order.)

Garden of Cosmic Speculation, by Charles Jencks, Frances Lincoln (2005)

Japanese Stone Gardens: Origins, Meaning, Form, by Stephen Mansfield, Tuttle Publishing (2009)

Labyrinths for the Spirit: How to Create Your Own Labyrinths for Meditation and Enlightenment,
    by Jim Buchanan, Gaia (2007)

Landscape as Spirit: Creating a Contemplative Garden, by Martin Hakubai Mosko and Alxe Noden,
    Weatherhill (2003)

Led by the Land, by Kim Wilkie, Frances Lincoln (2012)

Natural Companions: The Garden Lover's Guide to Plant Combinations, by Ken Druse (author), Ellen
    Hoverkamp (photographer), Stewart, Tabori & Chang (2012)

Open Spaces Sacred Places, by Tom Stone and Carolyn Rapp, TKF Foundation (2008)

Plant Dreaming Deep, by May Sarton, W. W. Norton & Company (1996)

Quiet Beauty: The Japanese Gardens of North America, by Kendall H. Brown (author),
    David M. Cobb (photographer), Tuttle Publishing (2013)

Sakuteiki: Visions of the Japanese Garden, by Jiro Takei and Marc P. Keane, Tuttle Publishing (2008)

Secret Teachings in the Art of Japanese Gardens: Design Principles, Aesthetic Values,
    by Donald A. Slawson, Kodansha USA, (2013)

Simply Imperfect: Revisiting the Wabi-Sabi House, by Robyn Griggs Lawrence, New Society Publishers (2011)

Stone, by Andy Goldsworthy, Harry N. Abrams (1994)

The Poetics of Gardens, by Charles W. Moore, William J. Mitchell , William Turnbull Jr., The MIT Press (1993)

The Wisdom of Trees: Mysteries, Magic, and Medicine, by Jane Gifford, Sterling (2001)

Wabi Sabi: The Art of Everyday Life, by Diane Durston, Storey Publishing (2006)

Zen and the Art of Pond Building, by D. J. Herda, Sterling (2008)

Zen Gardens: The Complete Works of Shunmyo Masuno, Japan's Leading Garden Designer,
    by Mira Locher, Tuttle Publishing (2012)

Selected Gardens and Places to Visit

Anderson Japanese Gardens
318 Spring Creek Road • Rockford, IL 61107
www.andersongardens.org

Arnold Arboretum of Harvard University
125 Arborway, Boston, MA 02130 98110
arboretum.harvard.edu

Berkshire Botanical Garden
5 Massachusetts 183, Stockbridge, MA 01262
www.berkshirebotanical.org

Bloedel Reserve
7571 NE Dolphin Drive, Bainbridge Isle, WA 98110
www.bloedelreserve.org

Botanical Gardens at Asheville
151 W.T. Weaver Blvd., Asheville, NC 28804
www.ashevillebotanicalgardens.org

Brooklyn Botanic Garden
1000 Washington Avenue, New York, NY 11238
www.bbg.org

Callaway Gardens
17800 US Hwy 27, Pine Mountain, GA 31822
www.callawaygardens.com

Chanticleer
786 Church Rd, Wayne, PA 19087
www.chanticleergarden.org

Chicago Botanical Garden
1000 Lake Cook Road, Glencoe, IL 60022
http://www.chicagobotanic.org/

Coastal Maine Botanical Gardens
132 Botanical Gardens Drive, Boothbay, ME 04537
www.mainegardens.org

Denver Botanical Garden
1007 York Street, Denver, CO 80206
www.botanicgardens.org

Dumbarton Oaks
1703 32nd St NW, Washington, DC 20007
www.doaks.org

Fairchild Tropical Botanical Garden
10901 Old Cutler Road Coral Gables, FL 33156
www.fairchildgarden.org

Frederik Meijer Gardens & Sculpture Park
1000 East Beltline NE Grand Rapids, MI 49525
www.meijergardens.org

Garvan Woodland Gardens
550 Arkridge Road, Hot Springs National Park, AR 71913
www.garvangardens.org

Golden Gate Park – Japanese Tea Garden
Golden Gate Park, San Francisco, CA
www.golden-gate-park.com/japanese-tea-garden

Grounds for Sculpture
18 Fairgrounds Road, Hamilton, NJ 08619
www.groundsforsculpture.org

Hakone Gardens
21000 Big Basin Way, Saratoga, California 95070
www.hakone.com

The Huntington Library, Art Collections and Botanica
Gardens
1151 Oxford Road, San Marino, CA 91108
www.huntington.org

Innisfree Garden
362 Tyrrel Road, Millbrook, New York 12545
http://www.innisfreegarden.org/

Little Sparta
Dunsyre, Scotland
www.littlesparta.org.uk

LongHouse Reserve
133 Hands Creek Rd, East Hampton, NY 11937
www.longhouse.org

Longue Vue House and Gardens
7 Bamboo Road, New Orleans, LA 70124
www.longuevue.com

Longwood Gardens
1001 Longwood Road, Kennett Square, PA 19348
www.longwoodgardens.org

Lotusland
695 Ashley Road, Santa Barbara, CA 93108
www.lotusland.org

Maymont Gardens
2201 Shields Lake Drive, Richmond, VA 23220

Meditation Mount
10340 Reeves Rd, Ojai, CA 93023
www.meditationmount.org

Memphis Botanic Garden
750 Cherry Road, Memphis, TN 38117
www.memphisbotanicgarden.com

Minnesota Landscape Arboretum
3675 Arboretum Dr. Chaska, MN 55318
www.arboretum.umn.edu

Missouri Botanical Garden
4344 Shaw Boulevard St. Louis, MO 63100
www.missouribotanicalgarden.org

Morikami Museum & Japanese Gardens
4000 Morikami Park Road, Delray Beach, FL 33446
www.morikami.org

Morris Arboretum of the University of Pennsylvania
9414 Meadowbrook Avenue, Philadelphia, PA
www.business-services.upenn.edu/arboretum

The Morton Arboretum
4100 Illinois Route 53, Lisle, IL 60532
www.mortonarb.org

Mountsier Garden (through Garden Conservancy
Open Days)
205 Rutgers Place Nutley, New Jersey
www.gardenconservancy.org/opendays

Naumkeag
5 Prospect Hill Rd, Stockbridge, MA 01262
www.thetrustees.org/microsites/naumkeag

New York Botanical Garden
2900 Southern Blvd., New York, NY 10458
www.nybg.org

Noguchi Museum
9-01 33rd Rd, New York, NY 11106
www.noguchi.org

Portland Japanese Garden
611 SW Kingston Avenue, Portland, OR 97205
www.japanesegarden.com

San Francisco Botanical Garden
Ninth Avenue and Lincoln Way, San Francisco 94122
www.golden-gate-park.com/strybing-arboretum

Sarah P. Duke Gardens
Duke University 420 Anderson St., Durham, NC 27708
www.gardens.duke.edu

Steinhardt Garden (through Garden Conservancy
Open Days)
433 Croton Lake Road, Bedford, NY
www.gardenconservancy.org/opendays

Storm King Art Center
1 Museum Rd, New Windsor, NY 12553
www.stormking.org

Tenshin-en Japanese Garden at Boston Museum
of Fine Arts
465 Huntington Avenue, Boston, MA 02115
www.mfa.org

Wave Hill
675 W 252nd Street, New York, NY 10471
www.wavehill.org

Acknowledgments

To all the teachers, designers and gardeners I have met in life and who have shared their knowledge with me, I wish to extend a big thank-you! I would also like to express my deepest thanks to all my friends who supported me throughout the writing, photographing, editing and design of this book.

Heaven is a Garden has been a long time in coming and would not have happened if I did not have the fantastic landscape design clients I have. Their glorious gardens make up most of the illustrations that are featured in this book. Since the best landscapes are the result of collaboration, I can truly say that my clients have guided me as much as I have helped them. We developed a vision together and worked, as a team, toward that goal. It is a special relationship that I treasure. I want to thank Marc and Rosemary, David and Melanie, Ted and Mary Jo,

Michael and Barbara, Edward and Maya, Tom and Cindy, Paul and Kim, Cole and Claire, Tom and Maureen, Guy and Diane, and Michael and Cheryl for allowing me to share photos of their gardens with others – and to my other clients whom I admire greatly.

I especially want to thank Laura McKillop, whose constant (almost daily) encouragement and enthusiasm sustained me when I needed it the most. Thank you for your kind ear, your horticultural reviews and your steady friendship. They were a writer's balm. You were the best cheerleader and support person I could have ever hoped for and I appreciate your creating those great diagrams at the 11th hour!

And two thumbs up for Catherine Dees, my editor, who was an early supporter and my guiding star. This book owes a lot to her keen intelligence and her insight. I am so happy that she is

a fellow traveler – it made our journey together so enjoyable. A big thank-you to the publisher of St. Lynn's Press, Paul Kelly, who took a chance when others wouldn't. And a giant and grateful hug to Holly Rosborough, whose artful eye and graphic skills made this the book that it is.

My love and thanks also go to my late father, John A. Johnsen, who instilled in me a love for art, gardens and design. He was a talented artist who taught me how to see and appreciate Nature from a young age. He took me on that fateful trip to the Japanese garden at the Brooklyn Botanical Garden, told me to "see the world, kid" and to never let rude reality get in the way of my dreams.

Last, but certainly not least, a big, loving thank-you to Rafael Algarin, my husband, for being my "rock" and partner through all these years. And to my son, Daniel, for being the light of my life and my constant joy. 🍂

About the Author

*J*an Johnsen is a highly regarded landscape designer, author and teacher, with a passion for plants and beautiful gardens. Having spent over four decades in the landscape profession, Jan loves to encourage others to see the opportunities that their plot of ground holds. She draws on her experience working in landscape architecture offices in Japan, East Africa, Hawaii, Vermont, New Orleans and New York to reveal little known secrets for creating great gardens. She shares these insights in her popular blog, "Serenity in the Garden," and on her Facebook pages, "Serenity in the Garden blog" and "Heaven is a Garden."

Known for her deep understanding of the beneficial impact of landscape design on our wellbeing, Jan is a sought-after speaker to groups around the country. She teaches at Columbia University and is an award-winning instructor at the New York Botanical Garden. Her garden designs have appeared in numerous magazines, including *This Old House, Landscape Architecture, Women's Day* and *Wallpaper*. She currently writes for *Garden Design Magazine*.

Heaven is a Garden is her third book. She is the proprietor, with her husband, Rafael Algarin, of Johnsen Landscapes & Pools in Westchester County, New York.

She cordially invites you to visit her at www.serenityinthegarden.blogspot.com.